# How to be a Pop Sensation

## The Ultimate Guide For Vocalists

By Pete Moody

Cover Design - Jacqui Perree
Cover Photography - Deryck Banks
(www.deryckbanks.co.uk)
With Thanks to - Emily Clare, Colin Hill

Gibson Publishing

First published in the UK by Gibson Publishing

How To Be a Pop Sensation
Text copyright 2010 by Peter Moody

ISBN 9780-9-567101-16

# Content

## Chapter One
# Introduction To Success

What will your friends say when they realise you have the knowledge and the power to really make waves in the music industry? This book will guide you through developing talent and give you the opportunity to get the break you deserve. You will learn techniques used by professional vocal performers and each simple step will increase your confidence, creativity and vocal competence.

Vocal performance experience is not required to benefit fully from the available techniques. Each chapter is in simple language, so it will not be necessary to learn about complex musical terms. Most importantly, this book will help you develop a great voice, so there is no need to worry about how you sound now.

Many readers may have already acquired some experience as a vocal performer. This book is for advanced singers as well as complete beginners. The techniques are new, exciting and beneficial to all. I have worked alongside many seasoned performers and opened the eyes of many other vocal teachers with the techniques I am about to share with you. Please do not underestimate the speed and simplicity of the techniques. They will turn a great voice into a sensational voice.

The term 'Pop' describes any music that is popular (favoured by lots of people). The techniques used here are suitable for all types of 'Pop' music including Musical Theatre, Rock, R&B, Garage, Soul, Rap, Swing, Easy Listening, MC and so much more. In order for you to increase your potential as a 'Pop Sensation' it is important to be individual and discover the unique sounds of which you are capable.

It may seem ideal to produce the same sound as your favourite performer, but there is no need for two identical performers in the charts.

Although you will be able to emulate the sounds of other artists, you will be exploring your own versatility and developing your own unique sound with the help of the techniques in this book.

Being a 'Pop Sensation' involves far more than just singing. The role also involves managing a busy schedule, allowing the world to follow you most of the time and being a role model for thousands of people. Think of performers that you enjoy.

These people have inspired you to become part of the music industry and you too will need to inspire and excite your audience. 'Pop Sensations' are in a very powerful position with each action potentially changing the lives of others. Hopefully successful artists created with the help of this book will have a positive impact on their audience.

Before going any further, you must become more focused and motivated than ever before. It is important to stay excited about your goals and enjoy every step you take toward them. Sit down and ask yourself "why do I want to be a 'Pop Sensation'?" Take some time to write a list of all your possible answers. This list will become the fuel for your motivation. You should try to make sure that you read the list every day.

By writing down your reasons, reading them every day and adding to them occasionally, you will always keep your goals in mind. Every time you read the list, you will feel excited and inspired to continue with your development. Picture all the positive things that success will bring. It will be yours one day.

## How to use this book

Regardless of current skill level, it would be advisable for anyone using this book to work through every chapter. It is important to practise each chapter until you are comfortable with the techniques shown. As well as being able to achieve the desired technique, you must also be able to understand how the technique works.

**As you practise, you should be able to agree with these statements:**
*"I am free of all struggle and strain"*
*"I feel no pain or tickling sensations in my throat"*

**You should also explore the following:**
*"What's happening to the sound?"*
*"How could I use this technique?"*
*"Why am I doing this?"*
*"How do I feel?"*
*"What can I feel happening?"*
*"Could I explain this technique fully to someone else?"*

You will be reminded of the above points throughout the book. They are your gauges to your level of understanding. When you feel you have mastered a section, move on to the next, but keep returning to previous sections. As a professional performing artist, practice should be continuous. Racing through the techniques will not allow you the time required to adopt the skills necessary to be a professional performer.

Every person's voice is very different. You may find it necessary to rework some chapters to strengthen specific areas of your voice or style. Having said this, at no point will any chapter become invalid. Each chapter contains specific instructions that should be followed exactly to gain maximum benefit. Please do not skip sections, as you will only be slowing your progress. Refer to the GLOSSARY at the end of the book if you are unsure of any technical terms used.

Keep this book in good condition - you will need to refer to it even as a professional singer!

## Practice makes closer to perfect

Anyone who believes that their performance leaves no room for improvement is perhaps not serious or knowledgeable enough about their art. Many thousands of muscles in the body require toning and conditioning regularly to achieve continued success. Conditioning these muscles must be a constant regime. As with exercising any part of your body, you would not expect it to retain stamina, condition or strength whilst not in use for a long period. Vocal performance requires the same level of commitment because muscles are involved.

Vocal fitness will be greatly enhanced by practising the techniques in this book on a daily basis. Don't worry, you do not need a jogging suit or sweat bands! The exercises you will be undertaking will gently tone your muscles and allow you to work comfortably at your own pace with no pain or strain of any kind.

Before you begin to practise, it is a good idea to find a space where you have privacy to work without fear of being interrupted or overheard. My favourite place to practise is in the car. With an extremely busy schedule, my travel time is usually the only time available to work on my own sound. It is also a good idea to practise at the same times every day. A time-based routine will be easier to stick to. If you just fit in practice here and there, whenever you can, you will find the practice becomes too much like interference in your life and your plans for success will be put on hold time and time again.

During practice, you will be experimenting with your voice, producing some strange sounds and making mistakes. This is what practice is all about. I frequently make mistakes and sound very peculiar during my vocal workouts. Remember, every time you make a mistake, you are one step closer to getting it right. Some of us need more steps than others but the results will always be worth the effort. For this reason it is a good idea to work in a space where you cannot be overheard. The last thing you need is the stress or embarrassment of wondering what others are thinking of you as you practise. Usually when you feel you are being overheard there is a tendency to work only the areas that are already comfortable to you. This will slow down your progress dramatically. Performance and practice are very different. You will not be experimenting with your voice during a performance and you should not have an audience during practice.

One of the questions mentioned earlier was 'how do I feel?' This question is vital to your continued success over time. We are going to look at emotional links to make your practice more enjoyable and productive. During periods of any emotion throughout our lives, we react to various stimuli, sometimes without even noticing them. Let's start by considering how some songs can make us feel and act differently. These songs will be different for every person.

There may have been a birthday party where a particular song was playing and we were feeling really happy. Although we may not even remember the song, our brain still dealt with that sound at the time. Years later we may hear the same song and start to feel happy. The song has been stored in our memory and attached to an emotion, often without us realising. All of our senses can link past emotion in our lives and create new emotional links. This happens every day.

With this in mind, it is important to feel happy, focused and motivated during each practice session. You will be able to use your 'why do I want to be a Pop Sensation' list to help you get into a positive, happy state of mind before you practise. If you are feeling depressed, or your stress levels are high, there is a risk of linking this emotion to your practice sessions. This will make your session hard work instead of enjoyable and your progress will be slow as a result. I want you to have the best possible chance of success. Happiness and motivation are the keys to achieving your goals.

Dealing with huge chunks of information can make completing tasks seem very daunting. The human brain can cope far better with small pieces of data which it has had time to process. It is advisable to read only a small section of a chapter at a time and work on any new exercises for no more than ten minutes before taking a break. Even while making a drink your brain will still be busy understanding and dealing with what you have just learned. Three ten-minute sessions will be more beneficial to you than half an hour of constant practice.

When all the techniques have been learned, practised and under-stood, you will be able to extend your practice time. Your brain will have already processed the information required. Everyone is different, but as a guideline I would suggest gradually building towards at least one hour of practice each day, which should ideally be split into two sessions.

## *Better safe than sorry*

I have already mentioned that practice involves conditioning the muscles in your body. As with any sport, if you have any medical condition or doubt about your physical ability to sing, then please consult with your doctor before you start to practise. If you feel any deterioration in your sound, due to even a simple head cold, then please allow proper recovery time before you commence further practice.

Overworking vocal muscles can cause damage to the voice. Incorrect technique may cause vocal weakness and slow your progress. Each exercise will guide you through the safest route to developing a great sound. It is important to read and under-stand the instructions before attempting any exercise. Your voice should be warmed up before it is used fully. Each vocal technique chapter will ensure your voice is gradually warmed up by simply working through the chapter exercises in order.

There are two main warning signs of voice damage for any singer. The first is pain and the second is a tickly or dry sensation. Both occur in the throat. If you feel either of these, then take a break, have a glass of water and do not start practice until these warnings have gone. Recovery time could be anything from half an hour to a week. If the problem persists, you should consult your doctor.

## *Something to remember*

Throughout my career, I have received countless pieces of wonderful advice from all sorts of people. I have also been knocked many times and told that my chosen career was nothing more than a dream. Many people have said: "you have to be so lucky to get that kind of job". Well, I have 'that kind of job' now. Luck is a real factor, but remember:

**"THE HARDER YOU WORK THE LUCKIER YOU GET"**

# YOUR NOTES

# YOUR NOTES

# YOUR NOTES

## Chapter Two

# Where's My Voice?

Every part of our personality and individual characteristics are shaped by past influences. This may be genetic or simply what we have been exposed to during our life. The way we walk, laugh or interact with others has been programmed into us. For example, if a person is born and raised in England, they will usually develop an English accent of some description.

Our natural instinct is to emulate personal characteristics from the many people we are exposed to as a child. It is a way of developing skills needed for adult life. During the whole of our lives, we also pass on good and bad thoughts and characteristics to others, often changing lives without realising it. With all this in mind, I am going to strip away some of your preconceived ideas and influences of singing to discover your truly natural voice hidden within.

During my many years as a vocal coach, I have listened to countless 'new' singers. Quite often, I hear great vocal qualities as singers chat about their goals and ambitions. It is when they begin to sing that most transform into a different person. The most common resulting sound could be described as either a 'half-baked' attempt at opera or a bad impression of Britney Spears. The reason for this transformation is simply that they TRY to be a singer. The brain has collected many pieces of information about singing and combined them to create a false understanding of what is required. These untrained singers are often attempting to recreate the sound of all of their favourite singers at the same time.

During this chapter you will develop a singing sound from speech to help you find the most natural route into vocal performance. The exercises will uncover both good and bad qualities in your voice. At this stage it is important to strip the voice right back to basics to ensure that you reap all the benefits of acquired techniques.

# Exercise One

Read the first paragraph of this chapter to yourself several times so that you become comfortable with each phrase. When you feel ready, read the same paragraph aloud. Practise this many times, so that you are able to deliver each line without hesitating or stumbling over your words. If you prefer, learn the paragraph well enough to recite without reading from the page, but still keep the paragraph close by in case you need a prompt at any point. The aim of this exercise is for you to deliver the lines naturally in your normal speaking voice. There should be minimum effort in your reading and it is important to be relaxed. Pretend you are speaking to someone who is sitting right next to you. Do not deafen them with too much volume.

During the next stages of this exercise, you will be altering the way you deliver the lines. The resulting sound will probably seem very unusual. Do not worry if this is the case. Read the first paragraph of this chapter again. This time try to remove all the gaps between the words of a sentence. You may only pause at a comma or a full stop. Stay relaxed and keep the reading at a slow pace. Do not change from a high sound to a low booming sound. Keep everything at the same level. There should be constant sound during each sentence. Many people find that the resulting sound becomes a drone or perhaps the style of delivery becomes unexciting or boring. If this is the case, you are carrying out the exercise correctly.

The last part of Exercise One involves stopping and holding the sound of part of a word. Choose any word from the paragraph and think about how the first syllable sounds. E.g. the start of 'WORD' sounds like 'WER'. The start of 'NATURAL' sounds like 'NA'.

Read the paragraph again without gaps between the words and stop on the start sound of the word you have chosen. Try to hold that sound for five seconds. At this stage, do not worry about the quality of the sound. Notice how easy and natural it is to create and sustain the sound without any more effort than speaking. This is your first big step into finding your voice.

Repeat this exercise using a different word in the paragraph. It is important that you do not increase the volume of this exercise, as this will take the sound away from its natural state.

**KEY POINTS**

* read the words over in your mind until you are familiar with them

* read the words aloud in a relaxed manner several times

* remove the gaps from between the words and deliver the lines

* choose a word to stop on and hold the sound for five seconds

* repeat this several times with different words

# Exercise Two

Now that you are comfortable with delivering a relaxed spoken sound, you can start work on a song, as opposed to a paragraph. Write out the first four lines of a favourite song. It does not matter what the song is. It could be anything from the latest chart hit to something as traditional as "Happy Birthday". Even if you know the words to the song really well, it will still be of benefit to write the lines down. When concentrating on technique, even the simplest words can be forgotten. Recap the KEY POINTS of Exercise One and repeat them with your song.

At this stage, you should be SPEAKING the words and NOT SINGING. The tune of the song should not be recognisable as you read. Now halve the speed of your reading. Reading in slow motion will allow you time to concentrate on the sound of each syllable. Remember to keep the volume low as you practise.

**KEY POINTS**

* apply techniques from Exercise One to a song

* halve the speed of the reading

During our every day conversations with friends and family, we change how high or low our voice is to inject meaning into each word. This is something we have learned during our life and has become so natural that we do not even have to think about it. These highs and lows (or pitch changes) are often as important as the words themselves. Now you will be experimenting with pitch changes so you may truly understand their value.

## Exercise Three

Say, "Why did you do that?" As you speak, think about possible reasons for asking the question. Repeat the question again in a deep, low voice. You will notice that it now sounds more aggressive. Now try the line again in a slightly higher voice. How does it sound? It may now sound more inquisitive or even frightened. This is an extreme example of spoken pitch changes. More subtle changes can be just as effective. Changes in spoken pitch are often referred to as 'inflections'. We change pitch in speech just as we do in song. Every conversation we have is filled with music. Try this exercise with other every day phrases.

### KEY POINTS

* say the question in a normal speaking voice

* repeat the question changing the pitch of your delivery

* repeat again altering the pitch once more

* experiment further with other phrases and pitch changes

## Exercise Four

As you read the lines of your song, start to change the spoken pitch of the words. To keep things simple initially, speak the first two words high and the next two low. Repeat this sequence through all of the lines. Pay particular attention to how high and low you allow the words to be. If the pitch is outside your normal spoken range then make some adjustments. You may find that the difference between high and low is very small or very large, and may even vary with each attempt. The result will be different for everyone. Your delivery of the lines should still be relaxed, not forced, but effortless. Once you are comfortable with this stage, spend some time experimenting by varying the sequence of pitch changes in your delivery. As long as your voice sounds natural and you are not singing, you may alter the pitch of every word or syllable.

**KEY POINTS**
* apply techniques from Exercise Two varying the spoken pitch

* change the sequence of pitch variation

# Exercise Five

Now for the first time we are going to think about the tune (melody) of the song you have chosen. Familiarise yourself with the melody of the song you have chosen by either going over the song in your head or playing the song on a stereo. Once you are happy that you can roughly remember the melody, read the lines again. As you read, try to pitch your voice to match the melody of the song. Don't worry about being 100% accurate at this stage. Remember you should not yet be singing, just speaking effortlessly. There will probably be a strong desire to sing out loud or even perform the song. Please resist doing this, as it will undo the work you have completed so far. Do not worry about the quality of the sound, enjoy the freedom of your natural voice and know that very soon it will become something to be proud of.

**KEY POINTS**
* familiarise yourself with the tune (melody) of the song

* speak the lines of the song adjusting the pitch of the words to roughly match the original melody

# Exercise Six

Now that you are able to work your spoken voice with a song, experiment with a variety of your favourite songs. Remember: do not allow yourself to sing the songs. No matter how energetic the song, keep relaxed and exert no more effort than you would do in a normal conversation.

**KEY POINTS**

  * apply techniques from Exercise Five to experiment with other songs

## *Make friends with your voice*

By now, you may love or hate the sound you are making with the exercises from this chapter. Practise these exercises for at least one week, or until you are confident with them, before moving on to the next chapter. This will allow you time to get used to your sound and for it to become a more natural experience. Be strict with yourself and try to avoid singing during this initial practice. As you progress through each chapter, you will be learning to shape and control this basic foundation sound. It will grow and evolve into something wonderful provided you give it the time and attention it deserves.

# Chapter completion checklist

Keep returning to the exercises in this chapter throughout your vocal development. You have successfully completed this chapter if you can agree with all of the statements below.

✓ I can explain why past influences may affect a singing voice

✓ I understand that my natural singing voice is closely related to my spoken voice

✓ I understand how spoken inflections relate to music

✓ I have not used a singing voice during this chapter

# YOUR NOTES

# YOUR NOTES

# Chapter Three

# Tuning Up

By now, you have discovered your basic natural voice. Your voice is a unique musical instrument that you will learn to look after and control. The sound that you have found during the last chapter will, from this point, be shaped and moulded into a professional musical tool. As with any instrument, you will learn to tune your voice to match other pitches and increase your ability to move smoothly from one pitch to another. Changing between different pitches will require your ears to work in conjunction with your voice to achieve maximum success. This section will help you pitch your voice successfully and will provide the exercises necessary to develop a musical ear quickly and easily.

Complex musical theory will not be required for you to master quickly the techniques for accurate, professional pitching. Each exercise is based on simply listening, remembering and repeating.

As we have already learned, we change the pitch of our voice every day during conversation. Let's take a moment to consider how we are physically able to do this. The many muscles in our voice box change position to alter how the air vibrates as it passes through. Sound, after all, is nothing more than vibrating air. When we sing a high note, the air vibrates at a very fast rate. A low note, however, is caused by a slower rate of vibration. Muscle movement causes very subtle sensation changes with each different note or sound we make. We will take some time now to experiment with, and experience, these subtle sensations.

## Exercise One

We will now gradually shift from speaking a sound to singing. Speak the sound 'zee'. Repeat this several times, ensuring that you are not exerting any more effort than you would for a quiet conversation. Once you are comfortable with your speech sound, start to hold it for a longer period. Gradually increase the time until you are able to voice the sound for around five seconds. At this stage, please check that your effort level is minimal and that the sound is quiet. Increase the volume of the sound slightly. The key word here is 'slightly'. We are aiming for a basic singing tone, still with minimal exertion. Do not be concerned with the quality and beauty of the tone. You are doing really well if you hold any type of sound steadily without straining or trying too hard.

Once you have practised this to your satisfaction then repeat, this time at a lower pitch. You do not have to try to sing the lowest note you can, just ensure the note is lower in comparison with your initial sound. When you are ready, try a higher pitched sound. Remember the usual rule applies – minimal effort.

Now you have practised three different pitches – regular, low and high. The sensations you feel in the back of your throat and/or your mouth will change very slightly with each different pitch. Practise moving from one pitch to another and concentrate on the different sensations that occur. The sensations will be very subtle so practise this pitch movement for at least ten minutes to get comfortable with the experience. If you are finding it difficult to notice any change in sensation, close your eyes and repeat the process. The sensations that occur are very slight. You will need to concentrate. Some people may find that they need to repeat the pitch movement for a short time each day to realise the sensations.

## KEY POINTS

* hold the sound 'zee' for five seconds

* increase the volume slightly, allowing yourself to gently sing the sound

* practise the same sound with a higher and lower pitch

* realise the subtle sensation changes that occur in your throat and/or mouth whilst singing at different pitches

# Exercise Two

By now, you have recognised slight sensation changes in your throat and/or mouth. This exercise will allow you to practise the sensations in relation to how your brain receives and processes sound. At no point during this exercise will you be making sound of any kind.

Close your eyes and imagine one of the three pitches made in exercise one. Think about the sound, and the sensation you felt, when you produced that pitch. Try to recreate that sensation now as you imagine the sound. You should feel like you are just about to sing a note. Your throat and mouth are ready for the sound to be produced. Again, there should be no tension, just anticipation. Concentrate now on a different pitch and prepare in the same way. Practise this several times. You are now beginning to become physically and emotionally prepared to create sound. In other words, you are learning the control required to make a sound in the way you want. From this moment on there will be no more 'hoping' that you make the right sound. If you prepare for the sound and imagine what it is going to be like then, with practice, you will get the pitch you want every time.

## KEY POINTS

* imagine a pitch but do not sing it

* recreate the sensation of the pitch in your throat and/or mouth

* recreate sensations of different pitches without making sound

During the previous exercises, you have learned to pitch single sounds/notes. A song will generally require you to correctly pitch and move between huge numbers of notes. This task may seem a little daunting at first but it is simply a case of breaking down sections of a song into short, manageable phrases where each single note can be practised. The following exercises will guide you through this process.

# Exercise Three

Select a song from your music collection and play it through from beginning to end. Choose one line from the song and write it down. It does not matter which part of the song your chosen line comes from. Listen to your chosen line at least five times, concentrating on each note. You may find, depending on your chosen song, that one word may be performed utilising many notes.

For example; the word 'voice', when spoken, usually results in a single note. However, in a song it may be performed over several notes i.e. voi-oi-oi-oi-ce. In this example, there are five individual notes or sound components to the single word. Pay particular attention to the number of notes in each word when practising your line. You may find it helpful to write the number of notes next to each word. If you are having difficulty counting individual notes, then clap the line through. Clapping each performed syllable will quickly enable you to identify the correct number of notes. If you are still in any doubt - work through the exercise with a friend.

Once you are clear about the number of notes, listen to the overall melodic pattern of the line. Does it start low in pitch and gradually get higher towards the end? Does it dip down in pitch in the middle? Listen to and think carefully about your chosen line. How does the pitch alter from beginning to end?

Turn off your music. Then, without singing, run through the line in your head and alter your vocal sensations (as in Exercise Two). Practise this until you feel confident that your anticipated notes match those of the song.

## KEY POINTS

* select a song and choose one line to work with

* listen to your chosen line at least five times

* carefully work out the number of individual notes in your line

* pay attention to the melodic pattern of your line

* silently practise creating the sensations required to sing the line

As we move toward delivering a line from our chosen song, it is important to remember that, at this stage, our primary concern is that we correctly pitch each note. Several factors may interrupt our ability to do this precisely. The main two obstacles are generally our hearing and our emotion.

When we recreate a musical note with our voice, we suddenly experience the need to recognise sound produced from within rather than from an external source. This complicates the listening process as we are hearing the internal sound, feeling the internal vibration whilst simultaneously monitoring the external sound quality. During Exercise Four, we will be simplifying the listening process and also removing obstacle number two – emotion.

I'm sure that we can all recall a time in our life when our emotions have got the better of us. Whether it's an angry outburst or an excited frenzy, emotions can alter the way we normally behave. Lyrics can create emotional links to the message of the song, the original artist, or our perception of a good performance. Although emotion is vital to a good performance, at this stage of learning we should be stripping this away to concentrate solely on accurate, basic musicality. Allowing emotion at this stage could result in a sound similar to a bad pub singer. Exercise Four will also provide a method to avoid this. We will be delving into the realms of adding emotion in later chapters.

## Exercise Four

Armed with your prepared chosen line, we can move on to the basic singing technique required for practising pitch. In order to remove some of the emotion derived from the lyrics, we are going to replace each syllable of the line with the sound 'dun'. E.g. 'High on a mountain top' would become 'Dun dun dun dun-dun dun'. There is less likelihood of emotional influences or performance comparisons with no real words. The 'D' sound at the start of 'dun' ensures that you sing the note quickly, with less chance of sliding the pitch. The 'n' sound at the end of 'dun' provides a vibration that is more easily monitored by our ears, thus improving the monitoring of the pitch.

For this reason, we must ensure that we constantly keep the sound 'dun'. When you start to practise, there may be a temptation to smooth the line by incorporating 'da' or 'di'. This will make pitching more difficult and we may miss mistakes. At this stage, we want pitching errors to stand out so they may be corrected from the start. Without the aid of your music, quietly and naturally sing the line with the 'dun' sound. If this is not pitched correctly, it may be necessary to repeat Exercise Three. Continue to practise the line but do not raise the overall volume any higher than that of a confident speech level.

**KEY POINTS**
* replace each syllable of your chosen line with the sound 'dun'

* avoid the temptation of 'da' and 'di'

* sing the line with 'dun' quietly and naturally

Now spend some time working on Exercises Three and Four with other lines and songs. Accurate pitching will make it far easier for your voice to blend with the backing music. This ability is vital and separates professional singers from karaoke singers. With this in mind, spend some time understanding the relationship between your instrument (the voice) and the other instrumentation in the song. Listen to guitar, bass and keyboard parts within your chosen song and emulate them with your voice. Work through Exercises Three and Four again, substituting the vocal line for different instrumental parts. Each time, be sure to sing each note to the sound 'dun'.

The 'dun' technique is a useful tool for any standard of singer. I can recall applying this technique to songs that I felt I knew extremely well, only to be hit with the realisation of inaccurate pitching.

Never fool yourself with the idea that you know a song too well to 'dun'. Even as an experienced, accomplished singer you will need to monitor your ability to pitch. Pitching is a skill that can slowly slip away and vanish completely without proper care and attention.

## Chapter completion checklist

Keep returning to the exercises in this chapter throughout your vocal development. You have successfully completed this chapter if you can agree with all of the statements below.

✓ I understand how vibration determines pitch

✓ I understand the relationship between the voice and ears when pitching

✓ I can create pitch sensations without sound

✓ I can interpret the number of notes in a song line

✓ I can interpret the melodic pitch pattern in a song line

✓ I understand that hearing and emotion can obstruct accurate pitching

✓ I can explain why the 'dun' sound is utilised in practice

✓ I can accurately pitch a line from my chosen song

# YOUR NOTES

# YOUR NOTES

# <u>YOUR NOTES</u>

# Chapter Four
# Get With The Beat

Every piece of music has life and a pulse. Just like our own pulse, the speed of the beats in a song can vary greatly and affect our overall experience. Even at a time of silent rest, our pulse continues to drive our very existence. The pulse of music works in very much the same way.

This chapter will enable you to identify the pulse (rhythm) of a song and ensure that your voice fits smoothly with, and adds to, the overall rhythmic pattern. Previously we looked at the importance of pitch and this, combined with rhythm, will provide you with the solid foundations on which to build your vocal style.

We already know that rhythm is, in its most basic form, the heartbeat of a song. Rhythm, like heartbeat, is measured over time and the overall speed of a song is usually referred to as a BPM value. BPM is an abbreviation for 'Beats per Minute'. For example, if a song had a BPM value of 60, we would expect a main beat count to occur every second. At 120 BPM, there would be two beats per second etc. If you have had the opportunity to watch a live band, the drummer will usually start a song vocally by setting the main beat speed for the benefit of the band.
E.g. "1, 2, 3, 4, 1, 2, 3, 4...etc"

This is not an alternative to 'ready-steady-go'; it is a count that will continue silently and often at the same pace throughout the piece. This basic count allows each player to work to the same timing.

By working at this common pace, musicians play in time with each other and start and stop at the right places. Individual notes vary in length but generally fit neatly on or between the main beat. As more notes are added at different points within the main beat, the rhythmic complexity increases.

For example, a drummer will usually play a different rhythmic pattern with each hand. This fits together around the main beat to create the overall rhythm. We will explore this further during the next exercises.

The above explanation will have given you some background information regarding rhythm. Rhythm is easier to feel than to talk about. Rhythm makes us want to dance. During the next few exercises, you will explore how to utilise rhythm and, after continued practice, you should start to feel rhythm rather than count it. Rhythm is a basic natural occurrence. Your breathing has rhythm. Your footsteps have rhythm and even your telephone's ring-tone has rhythm.

Counting main beats can vary depending on the style of the musical timing. Usually we count '1, 2, 3, 4, 1, 2, 3, 4…etc' (four-count), however, other styles (e.g. waltz) may be counted '1, 2, 3, 1, 2, 3' (three-count). There are many other variations on this.
The following exercises are all based on the four-count. The four-count is utilised in the majority of modern popular music. Once you begin to feel the rhythm, you will easily be able to adapt your vocal rhythms to fit other timings.

## Exercise One
During this exercise, you will practise counting a constant main beat. You will be counting '1, 2, 3, 4, 1, 2, 3, 4…' repeatedly. Each count must have the same time value as the last. Do not speed up or slow down your counting.

The ideal tool for this practice is a clock with a loud tick. If you do not have a clock of this type, then you should either hold a ticking watch to your ear or place your hand on the upper left side of your chest to feel the beat of your heart. First, identify that the ticks (or heartbeats) continue in a constant rhythm. Now start counting aloud making sure that your count is heard at exactly the same time as the tick. Try to make each '1' slightly louder than the other numbers. This four beat counting pattern is your main beat. You are now going to place other sounds on, and between, your main beat. Let us start with an offbeat. This means any sound that occurs at a different time to the main beat. We are simply going to add the word 'and' between the numbers (i.e. '1, and, 2, and, 3, and, 4, and, 1…'). Practise this until you are able to produce a smooth regular count along with the clock. Remember: only the numbers should fall on the tick. Also, try practising this part of the exercise with silent numbers (i.e. only speaking the 'and' between ticks).

To make the rhythm even busier, try adding three sounds between the numbers (e.g. '1, e, and, a, 2, e, and, a, 3, e, and, a, 4, e, and, a, 1…etc'). Once you are confident with this, experiment with making some components of the count silent.

**KEY POINTS**

 * use a clock or heartbeat as a marker for your main beat

 * count in time with the main beat making '1' slightly louder

 * add the word 'and' in between the numbers

 * add the sounds 'e' and 'a' to the rhythm

 * experiment by making some components of the rhythm silent

During the exercise, we voiced '1' slightly louder to mark the start of the pattern. This mark will become more useful when we apply the count whilst listening to our favourite songs. Do not panic if you find Exercise Two too difficult at this early stage. Return to it as necessary to develop your rhythmic recognition.

# Exercise Two

This exercise will help us identify the main beat of a song. Find a song from your music collection that includes drums. Drums often make the main beat more obvious to hear. Play the song and attempt to apply the four-count over the music. Each song is made up of lots of short rhythmic patterns and you must try to identify where each '1' count should start (it may not necessarily be at the start of the song). The start of each pattern should be slightly more obvious than the other counts and may be slightly louder. Some songs will be easier to work with than others and if you find this task difficult, try changing your chosen song.

Once you have established where each main beat occurs, choose one word from the lyrics. Then, using your experience from Exercise One, establish where your chosen word starts in the main beat count. Does it fall on or off the beat?

**KEY POINTS**
  * choose a song that incorporates drums

  * play the song and apply the four-count

  * if this proves difficult change your song

  * choose one word from your chosen song

  * investigate where your chosen word falls within the four count

As previously mentioned, drums often make the main beat more apparent. Drum rhythms are usually made up of a variety of percussive sounds. Individually, these sounds are usually very short. Our brain can identify and process short sounds much more quickly and accurately than longer sounds. In order to develop our rhythmic accuracy when singing, we should firstly translate the vocal part into something more percussive.

# Exercise Three
Clapping out rhythm helps us understand and process what we are about to sing. During this exercise, we will be replacing each syllable of the song words with a single clap. Play a song of your choice and write down the first line. Translate the line into claps per syllable. E.g. 'Under the velvet sky' would become 'clap-clap clap clap-clap clap'. Play the line of your song and clap along with the vocal rhythm. After repeating this several times, try to clap the rhythm without the song playing. Concentrating on just one line at a time, master the vocal rhythm of the entire song.

Think about how the different lines in the song compare when looking purely at rhythm.

**KEY POINTS**

* choose a song and write down the first line

* translate vocal syllables into claps

* practise clapping the rhythm along with the song

* learn the entire vocal rhythm of the song

* compare the rhythms of the different lines

Before jumping straight into singing the song through, we need to vocalise a short percussive sound to ensure our continued accuracy. The next exercise will be identical to Exercise Three apart from replacing the clapping with a vocal sound. The sound we will be using is 'bib'. Before we start, get used to the sound. The hard 'b' at the start of the sound creates a percussive-like quality, which can be punched from the lips. Make the sound as short as possible even when translating from a syllable that usually would have a longer duration. As you work through the exercise, keep your lips loose and relaxed for maximum effect.

# Exercise Four
Repeat Exercise Three replacing claps with 'bib'.

**KEY POINTS**

* translate vocal syllables into the vocal sound 'bib'

* practice 'bibbing' the rhythm along with the song

Now that the hard work is done, we can begin to sing our practised lines with the real words. Notice any areas of weakness and repeat exercises three and four as necessary to correct. As you have now witnessed first-hand, rhythm involves strict control of sound over time. So, how can we become more professional in our performance of rhythm?

The key to success in every performance art is to make it seem effortless. As far as rhythm is concerned, a common basic mistake is to give the impression that the music is controlling you. Even when performing to a backing track, this mistake can be avoided.

The final exercise in this chapter will challenge your ability to be comfortable with rhythm. For best results, a backing track (without original vocals) is better than practising along with the original artist, although this is not essential. Backing tracks, for popular songs in a variety of styles, can be purchased relatively cheaply in most music shops. Backing tracks will be of great benefit to your practice throughout all chapters. Challenging rhythm will be an important step in developing musicality and confidence. It will also provide you with the tools necessary to give the audience confidence in your overall control.

## Exercise Five

When singing a well-known song it is reasonably unnatural to alter the delivery from that of the original artist. For practice purposes, this is exactly what we will be doing. Start the song or backing track and sing the first word slightly late. This usually, even when expected, throws the brain into slight panic. There is often a desire to miss words or race to catch up with the original vocal rhythm. With this in mind, consciously and calmly adjust the rhythm of the line to take you from the error back into the usual rhythm smoothly. It does not matter how far into the song you get before you return to the usual rhythm. With practice, you will develop a calm, controlled approach giving you the freedom to play with vocal rhythm and appear more relaxed during performance. Repeat this exercise by also singing the first word early.

**KEY POINTS**

* sing the first word slightly later than usual

* calmly adjust the vocal rhythm to its correct position

* repeat again, now making the first word slightly early

# Chapter completion checklist

Keep returning to the exercises in this chapter throughout your vocal development. You have successfully completed this chapter if you can agree with all of the statements below.

✓ I understand rhythm and its purpose

✓ I can vocalise a main four-count

✓ I can demonstrate on-beat and offbeat occurrences

✓ I can recognise rhythmic patterns in a song

✓ I can reproduce a rhythm by clapping

✓ I understand that short sounds are processed easier than long sounds

✓ I can accurately deliver rhythmic vocal lines

✓ I can smoothly recover from rhythm errors

# YOUR NOTES

# YOUR NOTES

# YOUR NOTES

Chapter Five

# Air Flow

Every breath of air is potentially the raw ingredient for sounds we sing. As previously mentioned, sound is nothing more than vibrating air. Breathing, although a natural occurrence, is a process to be practised and understood in order to maximise the successful production of sound. Incorrect breath control can lead to a multitude of problems including vocal fatigue, inaccurate pitching, timing errors and can be a serious risk to the longevity and health of a vocal performer.

This chapter addresses fundamental breathing technique and outlines initial signs of incorrect breath control. Every professional singer should take breathing seriously and ensure that throughout their musical career, a strict practice regime is developed. Correct breathing is simple, effective and can be practised anywhere.

Very few people utilise all of their lung capacity. For this reason, be aware that your oxygen intake may increase during practice of this chapter. This extra intake may cause slight dizziness or lightheadedness. This is normal. However, you MUST stop and rest for a short while if the symptoms become more than a mild experience. If you have any form of respiratory ailment or medical condition, please seek advice from your doctor before continuing with the breathing exercises.

We are going to take a moment to experience airflow and its effect on a produced sound. This experiment highlights the effect of too little or too much air. When we speak or sing, breathing issues are usually less obvious than in this experiment. For this reason, it is important that we heighten our awareness to enable better control and diagnostics.

## The Air Flow Experiment
During this experiment, you will be required to whistle a single note. If you find whistling difficult then the same results can be obtained by using a shop bought whistle or similar air

to sound device. Clearly whistle a single sound. The duration of your sound should be around two seconds. Pay particular attention to the quality of your sound. At this stage, it should be clear and free from escaping air noise. Repeat your sound blowing as hard as possible. What do you notice? Usually there is additional unwanted escaping air noise and the pitch of your sound may change or fluctuate. These interferences occur in a similar way when we use too much air in singing. Repeat the sound again. This time blow as gently as possible. Usually, the sound stops and starts intermittently because the limited airflow is not providing enough support for a clear sound.

Now you are aware of the need to carefully balance air flow and monitor the resulting sound quality. Before you begin to exercise your breath control further, first ensure that you are taking air into your body in a controlled, effective way.

## Exercise One

Good posture is imperative for maximum breath control. Stand upright with your feet shoulder width apart. Relax your arms down by your side. Keep your head up straight and focus on an area in the room that is at natural eye level. Take a deep breath in and breathe out slowly. Pay particular attention to your shoulders. Shoulder movement does not help the breathing mechanism at all. Many people automatically lift their shoulders with a large intake of air. Make sure you do not do this. Let the weight of your arms keep your shoulders still. Continue to slowly breathe in and out and allow yourself time to get used to this upright, relaxed posture.

We are now going to maximise our air intake. You may have heard expressions like "to the diaphragm" or "breathe to the stomach". These expressions are fine if you can work out how to focus the air to those areas, but if not, here is a simple alternative explanation. Firstly, we need to identify the location of our sternum bone. This bone is often referred to as the breastbone. It is situated in the centre of our chest, its top is just below the neck, and the bottom is just above the stomach. Our ribs are attached to this central part of the rib cage. Just underneath the bottom of the sternum, above the stomach is a dip (no bone). With one finger, apply very light pressure to the dip. This pressure area is now a focus point to help achieve a full intake of air. Take a deep breath in and feel the expansion of air in your body creating slight pressure on the fingertip. You are now consciously taking air to the very bottom of your lungs. Breathe out slowly and repeat the exercise.

**KEY POINTS**

* stand upright with your arms relaxed by your side

* take deep breaths ensuring no shoulder movement

* locate the bottom of the sternum

* apply light pressure with a fingertip to the dip below the sternum

* take a deep breath in to feel added pressure on the finger tip

* breathe out slowly

Now we have practised maximising our breath intake we are now going to practise expelling the air in a controlled way. This process will require frequent practice to ensure consistent results. Every note we sing is the controlled flow of air passing through the vocal cords. In order to sing a pure, constant sound, our airflow must be controlled. If we get the airflow slightly wrong, we will suffer similar effects to those discovered in 'The Air Flow Experiment'.

# Exercise Two

As we work on the controlled expulsion of air, it will be necessary to prepare with a maximum intake of air (Exercise One). We will be letting the air escape to the sound of 's' (phonetic), just like a hiss. Concentrate on the level and variation of your 's' sound. The perfect airflow at this stage should last around five seconds and not waver in any way. Keep the sound volume low as you practise this. As you become competent at maintaining a smooth hiss, gradually extend the length of sound time. If you are unable to keep the sound constant, try creating slight tension in the stomach area. Once you are confident with the exercise, practise letting out a minimum amount of air with an almost silent hiss. Less air escaping enables longer output, but requires more control. Accomplished singers should be able to maintain a comfortable, smooth silent output for thirty-seconds without any strain. DO NOT hold the output for any longer than comfortable. Remember we are controlling breath for singing, not deep sea diving!

This exercise can be practised anywhere and you should try to practise for at least ten minutes per day. Most people should be comfortably reaching a thirty-second output time within approximately two weeks.

**KEY POINTS**
  * prepare a full intake of breath (Exercise One)

  * slowly let air escape to the sound of 's' (hiss)

  * maintain a steady flow of air without wavering

  * reduce the hiss volume

  * increase your smooth output time gradually

We all know that air is vital to our existence. As a result, there is often a tendency to gasp for air in between the lines of a song or rush the rhythm in order to finish a line and take some more air in. These are both traits of a bad performer and demonstrate lack of preparation to the audience. During the next exercise, you will be transferring your knowledge and control of airflow to a song.

# Exercise Three

Write down the words to a song of your choice. As you work though this exercise, you will be developing experience in adopting a constant approach to breathing. One of the main reasons for gasping or rushing during a song is simply because we may approach it differently each time. With this in mind, slowly sing through your song, placing a tick-mark against the lyrics wherever a breath is required. Try to avoid placing a tick-mark halfway through a word. Work through the song at least three times before you decide on the definite placement of ticks. From now on, you will follow your own written instructions as to where a breath is required. Each performance will now have the same constant approach as far as breathing is concerned.

For practice purposes only, you will now be singing every other line in the lyrics. This gives you the luxury of plenty of time to relax and prepare breath for the smooth delivery of words. Some songs, especially upbeat songs, do not give us enough time to prepare breath adequately. As you practise, occasionally swap between starting lines of the song to ensure that you work with all the lyrics. Once you are comfortable with your breathing, include all lyrics, but still maintain a relaxed, refreshed approach to each new line. In other words, treat each line of a song as though it were the first.

## KEY POINTS

* write out the lyrics of the song

* place a tick mark against the lyrics wherever a breath is required

* practise singing every other line to allow more space in the song for correct breathing

* sing the entire song treating every line as if it is the first

I am often asked, "How much air should I give each word?" Unfortunately, there is no definitive answer for this. The delivery of words varies from song to song and we all manage air flow in a slightly different way, depending on our voice type. A better question to ask would be, "How little air can I create a good sound with?" During the next exercise we will investigate this. We tend to allow far too much air per sound than we need to. This is our natural safeguard against a subconscious belief that we may run out of air and feel faint.

In order to manage this subconscious belief we must prove to ourselves that we can create quality sound with minimum air. In the long term, this will make us efficient singers with the ability to carry sound over longer periods. In general, lower pitch sounds require slightly more air than higher pitches.

# Exercise Four

We are going to pitch two different sounds. We need to create one high sound and one low sound. Both should be comfortable and sung without stress or strain. For practice purposes, use the sound 'doh' for both pitches. Hold the lower pitched sound without wavering for as long as you are able. As soon as any wavering starts, attempt to sing the higher pitch straight after the low pitch without an extra breath. You should find that the higher pitch is relatively easy to achieve with minimal air. Reverse and repeat the exercise starting with the high note. This may prove slightly more challenging. Practise this exercise daily in order to improve your ability to create quality tones with minimal air.

### KEY POINTS

* practise singing a high and a low-pitched sound

* hold the low pitch as long as possible

* without taking an extra breath, sing the high pitch directly after the low pitch

* reverse the exercise, so that you start with the high pitch

## *Increasing Natural Resonance*

When we take a large inward breath, our body expands and this opens up more space for resonance to occur. Shallow breathing can lead to resonance from only the neck up, which gives less warmth and fullness to the tones we sing. The following exercise will help you realise the importance of opening up your body with air when you sing. If possible, record a line or two of a song before trying this exercise and then again afterward to compare the quality of the tone. Only attempt Exercise Five if you are fully fit and healthy as it involves balance and moderate physical exertion.

# Exercise Five

This exercise will allow you to feel air filling your body and give you another focus point in which to direct your breathing. You will be required to balance on one leg during this exercise, so please ensure you have something to support yourself with should you lose balance.

Stand with your feet shoulder width apart and take a few deep breaths (as previously directed in early exercises). Lift one knee toward your chest and hold it in position with one or both hands. Try to lift the knee as high as is comfortable. With your knee lifted and held tight, take a deep breath in. You will feel a slight pressure on your lower back as you breathe in. This pressure feels almost as if the air is flowing all the way to your lower back. Once you are happy that you are experiencing this pressure, stand normally and try to create the same sensation whilst breathing in. This 'opening up' exercise is a good way to start your practice sessions as it encourages deeper breathing and prepares the body to be resonant.

## KEY POINTS

* stand and take several deep breaths

* lift one knee high toward your chest and breathe in

* notice any pressure sensation around your lower back

* try to feel the same sensation standing normally and breathing in

If you have any problems with controlling the correct amount of breath during a song, try reducing your store of air before attempting a line. Do this by taking in the full amount of air and releasing some before you start the line. This will enable you to maintain a good breathing technique whilst you experiment with your air-flow levels. Your general fitness level may also have a great effect on your ability to use air economically. If you are relatively unfit, it may be worth considering complementing your singing practice with an exercise regime. Consult your doctor for advice and guidance on exercise that is suitable for you.

# Chapter completion checklist

Keep returning to the exercises in this chapter throughout your vocal development. You have successfully completed this chapter if you can agree with all of the statements below.

✓ I understand that sound is vibrating air

✓ I have experienced the effect of too much or too little air during 'The Air Flow Experiment'

✓ I can breathe in successfully to the base of my sternum

✓ I can breathe out in a controlled unwavering manner

✓ I understand the benefit of tick marks against lyrics

✓ I prepare my breathing for every line I sing

✓ I have experimented with the amounts of air required for quality sound

✓ I can open up my body's resonance

✓ I understand that my overall fitness may affect my singing

# YOUR NOTES

# Chapter Six

# Vibration Station

The voice is a unique instrument. We all have a wealth of wonderful undiscovered sounds within us. With some simple knowledge and experimentation, we will begin to unlock our real singing voice. As the sound of our voice vibrates through our body, singing becomes an experience rather than just sound. Creating quality sound involves the whole body and a single note has the potential to take you and your audience on an emotional journey.

When we sing, sound resonates around different parts of our body in the same way that the body of an acoustic guitar amplifies and embellishes the sound quality of the vibrating strings. We are a live soundboard. Unlike a guitar, we have more than one area in which to direct resonance. We call these areas 'Resonating Cavities'. Resonance is the perceived quality of sound in a space, e.g. singing in the bathroom will sound different to singing in the living room because the space around us is different in size and materials. During this chapter, we will discover how to consciously make use of resonance within our body and become a vibration station!

Resonance is not something completely new. Whenever you make a sound it is resonated, to some extent, in your body. This gives your spoken voice the quality and texture that you are familiar with and use every day. Changing or redirecting the space (your resonating cavity) may at first, seem quite unnatural and strange. Please practise and allow yourself to become familiar with other usable cavities. Like anything new, unfamiliar resonance may take some time to get used to and control correctly. The results are worth the practice.

Let us create an external resonating cavity so that we can understand and experience what may be occurring in your body later in the chapter.

# Exercise One

During this exercise, you will need to pay particular attention to vibration and sound alteration. Cup your hands together in front of you with palms up. The empty cupped space is going to become our resonating cavity. Sing and hold a steady note. Make your note reasonably low in pitch. In order to hear clearly the effect of the cavity, it is important to maintain the same unwavering pitch throughout the exercise. Bring your cupped hands up to your face with your mouth and nose in the cup. As you hold the note, listen to the effect of your cupped hands. Alter the shape of the cup slightly whilst holding the note and listen to how the sound changes with the shape of your cupped hands. Because this resonating cavity is part of your body, you will be able to feel a slight vibration on your hands as you sing. This vibration is quite subtle, but it is the key to aiming your voice into different parts of the body. As we use internal resonating cavities, we will feel similar vibration in other parts of our body.

**KEY POINTS**

* cup your hands, palms up, in front of you

* hold and maintain a steady note

* raise up your cupped hands to cover your mouth and nose

* listen to the change in quality of the note as you alter the shape of your hands

* feel the vibrating sensation caused by the sound on your hands

You now understand a little more about resonating cavities and their effect on sound. During the remainder of the chapter, we will be focusing on three main internal cavities and learning to direct sound to them. The cavities are CHEST, HEAD and MOUTH.

Most people, including many famous vocal performers, tend to focus on only one resonating cavity for their sound. This is usually due to preference, natural tendency or quite simply lack of knowledge. As a professional performer, it is important to experience and cultivate the effect of all cavities. Effective cavity use will arm you with the capability of being a far more versatile performer. You may decide that your voice suits one cavity more than the others do, but this decision should only be made after mastering all areas.

During everyday speech, we actively utilise at least one resonating cavity. By the end of the chapter, you should determine which of the main three cavities you place your voice toward naturally. This will aid your overall understanding of the voice and highlight unfamiliar territory that you need to practise more.

## *Chest Cavity*

The chest cavity is generally the easiest to work with first, because the results are slightly easier to feel than the other areas. The space behind the top of your rib cage (chest) will be the area of resonance. This space is large and, in comparison to our cupped hands, results in a deeper, warmer vocal sound. Many singers naturally make use of the chest cavity when performing low notes. However, contrary to popular belief, it is also possible to direct higher notes to the chest too.

Let's experience the basic feeling that comes from resonating sound around the chest area. The following exercise is only an introduction. Subsequent chapters will reiterate and expand upon this exercise to deepen your understanding of chest cavity application.

# Exercise Two

Stand in a comfortable upright position. Sing and hold a low note to the sound of 'argh'. Depending on your natural voice type, you may already feel some subtle vibration occurring around the chest area. To create a focus point and heighten your awareness of the vibration, place either hand at the top and centre of your chest (just below your neck). Your palm should be against your chest. Repeat the same note to experience the vibration again. Now alternate between a high note and a low note. You should experience less vibration as you sing the higher note. This occurs simply because low notes are naturally directed toward the chest resonating cavity. Repeat the exercise with your eyes closed in order to 'feel' the vibration and create an emotional link to the experience. Remember, the vibrations can be very subtle. Do not worry if you do not feel any vibrations straight away as it may take a little practice to be aware of this.

**KEY POINTS**

* stand upright

* sing a low note to the sound of 'argh'

* place your hand flat against the top of your chest

* feel the vibration

* alternate between high and low notes

* feel the vibration intensity alter

* repeat the exercise with your eyes closed

This may be your first conscious experience of sound resonating within your body. As you progress through chapters, you will learn to alter your sound quality and focus. You will be able to direct any sound to resonate within the chest and develop technique to maximise the warmth and depth of your sound.

## *Head Cavity*

No prizes for guessing which part of your body will experience vibration here (the head!). The space at the back of the throat and roof of the mouth is the resonating area. This also causes slight vibration of the skull. In contrast to the chest cavity, the head cavity is most easily utilised when performing high notes. With correct, controlled use of the cavity, it will also be possible to direct lower notes to this area.

Use of the head cavity should result in a strong, pure tone. Taken to the extreme, this pure tone is like that of an amplified tuning fork or an opera singer attempting to break glass! Don't worry, your windows should be safe as you work through this book, but you may experience any loose objects in the room vibrating and rattling slightly when you achieve the perfect head cavity sound. This entirely depends upon where you practise.

The head voice is slightly more difficult to experience than the chest voice. Please remember that the following exercise is simply the introduction. Do not panic if you have trouble with this exercise. As with the chest cavity exercise, you will have plenty of opportunity to practise, develop and understand this technique fully in subsequent chapters.

## Exercise Three

During this exercise, you will be producing SHORT bursts of reasonably LOUD sound. Closely follow the instructions and practise this exercise for no more than five minutes per day. Incorrect or prolonged use of this cavity may cause discomfort. It is important to emphasise the need to stop practice for at least one hour if any uncomfortable sensations occur within your throat.

Stand with your feet shoulder width apart and relax your shoulders. Your head should be raised slightly and facing straight ahead. You may find it useful to focus on a fixed object within the room to help maintain correct posture throughout. Visualise a high note and prepare your throat to create the sound. You will be producing a very short, loud, 'oi' sound. To help you visualise the sound, imagine someone has just stolen something from you and is now running away with it. Your 'oi' sound needs to be strong enough to raise the attention of others and demonstrate, to the imaginary thief, that you are angry. As you produce the sound, your jaw will drop to create an open mouth shape. Practise this sound a few times. Ensure that there is no discomfort as you do this. Remember, you are producing an assertive strong sound, not screaming!

Only move on to the next part of the exercise when you are happy that you can create a short, strong sound without any strain or struggle.

Now you have experienced the type of sound required for this exercise, you should be able to recreate it at a slightly lower volume. This will eliminate any risk of fatigue or strain. We are now going to extend the sound so that it lasts for no more than three seconds. Resume the correct stance and close your eyes whilst holding the sound. Try to feel where the sound is vibrating in your body and gently touch different parts of your face and head to help highlight any vibration felt. If you do not feel any vibration straight away, try slowly altering the shape of your mouth from wide (like a smile) to open (like a yawn) until you achieve the best sound quality. Although awareness of vibration in the head or face is a key indicator of success here, also be aware that the sound you make should feel good. If you are creating a loud, pure sound easily with little effort, then you are on your way to developing a great head resonant sound.

**KEY POINTS**

* stand upright

* close your eyes

* sing a reasonably loud 'Oi' Sound

* when comfortable with the sound, hold it for three seconds

* use your hands to help feel any vibrations as they occur

* alter your mouth shape to create the best result

## Mouth Cavity

The resonating space in your mouth can be utilised in a variety of ways. For the purpose of this introduction, we will be learning how to alter a sound within this resonating space. The mouth resonating space is one of the key areas we should develop to create a modern Pop/Rock sound. We can liken this cavity to an effects processor. Once we create a sound in our larynx, we can then add extra dimension and texture through using our mouth as a filter or controller of the sound. The Mouth Cavity is often used to purify or to create a brighter, more complex texture to our sound. As with the other resonating areas, you will experience the basics of the mouth cavity using the following exercises. We will experiment further with this cavity in subsequent chapters.

# Exercise Four

This exercise allows you to play with the sounds that you have learned to create in previous chapters. It will introduce you to the concept of mouth space. You will develop mouth cavity resonance in the next chapter.

Stand with your feet shoulder width apart and relax your shoulders. Your head should be raised slightly and facing straight ahead. Sing any comfortable, relaxed note to the sound of 'oh'. Repeat this until you are comfortable that the sound is unwavering and you can hold it for five seconds. As you hold the note, your mouth should be naturally open and rounded in the shape of an 'o'. As you continue holding the note, gradually and slowly change the shape of your mouth to become more like a smile and you should finish with your teeth together. You will notice that the sound alters slightly as you change the shape of your mouth. You may also experience some vibration occurring around your teeth and cheeks. Repeat the sound again and this time, raise and lower your jaw as if you are chewing gum. This should not only alter the sound but will also affect the volume. With your jaw lowered, you will notice a louder sound. Repeat this entire exercise with the sounds, 'ee', 'a' and 'ung' (as in young). Notice the different vibration and sound qualities achieved by each sound. During the practice of 'ung', you will probably experience a more nasal quality to the sound. This is perfectly normal and is something that we will develop further in subsequent chapters.

**KEY POINTS**
* stand upright

* sing any comfortable note to the sound of 'oh'

* change the shape of your mouth as you hold the note

* repeat the sound whist raising and lowering your jaw

* repeat the entire exercise with 'ee', 'a' and 'ung'

With practice, the introductory exercises in this chapter should lead to a realisation of the potential we have for altering sound quality. Ensure that you understand the importance of feeling a produced sound as well as hearing it. It may be necessary to work with these exercises frequently in order to experience the vibration that occurs around the body with each of the techniques.

## Chapter completion checklist

Keep returning to the exercises in this chapter throughout your vocal development. You have successfully completed this chapter if you can agree with all of the statements below.

✓ I understand that sound resonates in a space

✓ I understand and have felt that vibration occurs around the body when I sing

✓ I can name the three main resonating areas

✓ I have experienced vibration in my head when producing a high sound

✓ I have experienced vibration in my chest when producing a low sound

✓ I have noticed that my sound quality/volume alters depending on the shape of my mouth

# Chapter Seven
# Vocal Effects Unit

Every 'high-tech' recording studio is equipped with countless gismos and gadgets to improve and alter the sound quality of any recorded noise. During this chapter we will be learning to shape, improve and develop our sound, naturally using the body's own vocal effects unit (the mouth). Through developing and practicing to utilise this vital singing component, we not only greatly improve our versatility but also develop a professional approach to singing. We will discover the impact of the vocal effects unit on both performance and general microphone technique.

Let's start by looking at a very basic example of how simple mouth shapes can affect delivery of sound and also impact on an audience. Imagine yourself back in a school assembly, watching a presenter at a conference or even attending a church service. If you are standing at the back of the room and the person speaking is at the front, there is every chance that you may have to strain, struggle and literally force yourself to listen. Inevitably this will have a great impact on your concentration level. If the person speaking does not move their mouth very much when delivering the speech, your chances of staying focused drop considerably. There are a number of reasons for this. First, and most obviously, we all have some ability to lip-read and our brain balances what we see and what we hear and attempts to provide us with a logical interpretation of both.

Another reason for not staying focused in this situation is the clarity and volume of the speaker. With little mouth movement occurring, the person speaking is actually muffling the sound of their own voice. This has a negative effect on audience concentration and breaks the first rule of successful use of the vocal effects unit.

Good mouth shaping is the most basic, yet most effective technique to improve a voice within minutes (singing or spoken). Let's consider another example. Imagine someone is playing a trumpet. The sound quality is rich, loud and pure. If you were to take the trumpet and hammer the end into a different shape, you would obviously expect to hear a different sound when it is played again. The same principle applies when we change the shape of our mouth. You will have experienced some of this sound alteration in the previous chapters. Let's now look at how to apply these shapes to a song.

There are two main shapes for us to apply. The first is a very open 'operatic' shape that is vertical and open. The second is a wide horizontal shape that is similar to an extreme, 'teeth together' grin. The choice of which shape to use depends entirely on the material you are singing and the desired quality of sound we want to achieve. The first step to applying shape is to understand a little about vowel sounds (a, e, i, o, u).

E.g.

> 'a' as in 'apple' 'a' as in 'a Singer'
>
> 'e' as in 'egg' 'e' as in 'ee'
>
> 'i' as in 'insect' 'I' as in 'I am'
>
> 'o' as in 'orange' 'o' as in 'oh'
>
> 'u' as in 'umbrella'

Vowel sounds are different from traditional vowel use. We identify the vowel sound in a word by the way we hear it, rather than the way it is spelled, (e.g. Sky has the vowel sound 'i', even though the letter 'i' does not feature in the spelling). You may have noticed that 'u' is missed out from the second column list of vowels. This is because the sound 'u' is made up of other vowel sounds and is expressed as 'ee-oo'. Let's use this knowledge to experiment with vowel sounds.

# Exercise One

During this exercise, you will be experimenting with the effect of mouth shape on a vowel sound. Let's start by singing the vowel sound 'a' (as in 'apple'). The sound should be sung at a slightly higher pitch than speech and held for approximately five seconds. Sing the sound using a horizontal mouth shape and then repeat with a vertical shape. You will experience a difference in the sound quality of each shape and find that one shape is more comfortable and natural. Using the example of 'a', you may find that the vertical shape sounds more operatic than the horizontal shape. The horizontal shape tends to be brighter and perhaps more suited to a rock/pop genre. This experience of shape will change depending on the vowel sound that is being sung. Repeat the exercise with all the vowel sounds. Remember to over-exaggerate the shapes as you practise, this will help you become more accustomed to this seemingly unnatural, yet crucial, approach to delivering sounds.

**KEY POINTS**

* practise with over-exaggerated mouth shapes

* sing the vowel sound 'a' (as in apple) using a horizontal mouth shape

* repeat with a vertical mouth shape

* monitor the effect created by the different shapes

* repeat with all the vowel sounds

The following exercise will enable you to make the most of each word (and its component syllables) in a song of your choice. If you have the luxury of a recording device, it would be wise to record yourself singing a couple of lines from your chosen song before applying the technique from the next exercise. It is sometimes easy to underestimate the power of good shaping and I am sure you will be amazed at the difference when you listen back to a before and after recording.

## Exercise Two

During this exercise, you will be working with a small section of a song of your choice. Even if you feel you know the lyrics really well, it is advisable to have a written copy available to work from during this exercise. First, you need to work out which shape should be used for each word (or syllable) of the song. You will be able to do this based on the previous experience acquired during 'Exercise One' of this chapter.

Circle every vertical shaped sound on the lyrics (with a pencil as you may change your mind!) and underline every horizontal shaped sound.

E.g.

**(Open)(your) eyes and see my (love)(to)day**

Now sing the prepared lyrics ensuring that you over-exaggerate the shapes. You may find it easier to slow down your singing until you grow accustomed to shaping the sound. Do not be concerned if this approach feels unnatural. Continue working with your chosen lyrics until you are happy that the shapes are the right ones for the sound required.

### KEY POINTS

* choose a small section of a song of your choice

* prepare a written copy of the lyrics

* circle vertical words and syllables

* underline horizontal words and syllables

* practise singing the lyrics using your predefined mouth shapes

* experiment by changing the shapes until you find the most suitable approach

This exercise provides you with a proven formula for ensuring that each note that you sing is given individual time and attention. It is very easy to sing a line of a song and feel that it is adequate. Please get into the habit of making every millisecond of sound the very best it can be. The following exercise is often used as a fast-track version of the above. It should be used to assist you to quickly find the most natural shape for a sound and help you plan your vocal performance.

## Exercise Three

This exercise will quickly help you to discover how mouth shapes contribute to a new level of vocal clarity. The following should be practised with every song that you perform. As with every other vocal technique, it is best to work on small sections of a song to ensure full attention is given to every lyric. As with 'Exercise Two', choose a small section of a song that you wish to perform. Gently sing the words with your teeth held tightly together. You are now relying purely on mouth shape to make each word understood. If you are not shaping each sound correctly, the result will be similar to the sound of a bad ventriloquist.

Correct shaping will allow the words to be clearly understood, even though your teeth are together. After several minutes of practice, you should notice that your cheeks and face begin to ache slightly. When this happens, stop practising and return to the exercise later. This slight ache proves that you are using your facial muscles much more than you usually would. With time, you will be able to shape sound in this way without feeling any muscle fatigue.

**KEY POINTS**

* choose a small section of a song of your choice

* perform the section whilst keeping your teeth together

* rely entirely on mouth shape to gain clarity

* stop practising this technique if/when you feel any muscle ache or fatigue

Mouth shape also has a big impact on the air that is expelled when we sing. When using a microphone, we should not allow lots of air to get in the way of our sound. It is for this reason that many recording studios use a device called a 'POP SHIELD'. Pop shields are a circle of thin, close-netted material (similar to the material used in women's tights), which is held in a frame. This is placed in front of the microphone and helps prevent air from affecting the recorded sound. If air blows hard from our mouth as we sing, especially on any 'b' and 'p' sounds, then this can sound like a gust of wind or a loud pop on the recording.

As singers, we can reduce and even eliminate the need for a pop shield by correctly producing sound with the appropriate mouth shape. The following exercise is designed to assist you monitor the extent of harsh airflow and begin to control it.

## Exercise Four

Whilst practising this exercise, you must continue to over-exaggerate your mouth shapes. Your microphone technique will be developed, but you will not be required to practise this with a microphone. A more detailed explanation of microphone technique is covered in the 'Microphone Technique' chapter.

We will be simply using our hand as a harsh-air monitor. Read the first sentence of this paragraph aloud with your hand held flat in front of your mouth. Your palm should be about two inches from your lips. You will notice air hitting your palm as you speak. There will be an extra harsh burst of air as you say the word 'simply'. This is due to the hard 'p' sound. 'P' causes the most 'popping' of all of the sounds you can make.

Repeat the sentence and experiment further with the shape of your mouth as you read. You will notice that some shapes disperse the air much better than others do. Your aim is to read the entire sentence with a minimum amount of air hitting your palm. Repeat the exercise with lines from your favourite song and notice that the clarity improves in proportion to the reduction of air.

**KEY POINTS**

- ✴ place your hand flat in front of your mouth

- ✴ your palm should be approximately two inches from your lips

- ✴ read the first sentence of 'Exercise Four'

- ✴ notice extra air hitting your hand as you say 'simply'

- ✴ experiment with mouth shapes to achieve clarity and reduced airflow

- ✴ repeat the exercise using lyrics from a song

Now that you have experimented with mouth shapes and the effect they have on sound, let's look at taking advantage of the vertical and horizontal approaches to solve future performance issues. You hopefully discovered some basic patterns emerging whilst you matched vowel sounds to shape, e.g. 'o' is mostly vertical and 'e' is mostly horizontal. Vertical and horizontal also create very different textures to our voice. We can mix and match these textures and where necessary, alter vowel sounds of a word to our advantage.

For example, if you sing the words 'just because'. The 'ee' sound in 'because' makes you naturally perform this with a horizontal shape. However, if you would prefer to have the purer, more rounded, sound of a vertical shape then you can alter the vowel sound of the word without making it sound wrong to the audience's ears. 'Because' can become 'bay-cause'.

This may seem a little strange at first, but with careful practice, your audience will not even notice the change in vowel sound. Likewise, if we start with a vertical sound like 'door' but would prefer to have a brighter horizontal sound, we simply alter the vowel sound to 'daw'. Experiment with the lines of your chosen song to see if any vowel sound changes would be beneficial.

I hope that you are now aware of the potential of your 'vocal effects unit'. Keep experimenting with shaping every syllable and remember that when you sing a sound that feels good, it usually sounds good too. In my own practice sessions, I can spend over an hour playing with and shaping just one syllable. Play with sound as often as you

# Chapter completion checklist

Keep returning to the exercises in this chapter throughout your vocal development. You have successfully completed this chapter if you can agree with all of the statements below.

✓ I understand that mouth shape affects sound

✓ I understand the impact of correct and incorrect shaping on an audience

✓ I am able to produce vertical and horizontal sounds

✓ I can hear and feel the difference between vertical and horizontal sounds

✓ I can apply shaping to any sound

✓ I can also use shapes to improve microphone technique by controlling expelled air

✓ I can change vowel sounds of a word to improve my performance

## Chapter Eight
# Soulful Singing

During this chapter, we will be focusing on the creation and development of a 'soulful' sound. The definition of soulful singing is the ability to create a rich, warm and thick texture to your sound. This will add depth to your voice and provide another sound tool to add to your repertoire. Soulful singing is not purely geared toward soul music. The technique can be used to great effect across many genres of music.

Soulful singing makes great use of the CHEST RESONATING CAVITY. It may be worth revisiting the introduction to the chest cavity, which was outlined in Chapter Six. It is important to understand the reasons why sound is perceived as: deep, warm, thick. These descriptions are often referred to as indicators of texture. Imagine a variety of different musical instruments: guitar, piano, trumpet, flute. If these instruments played exactly the same musical note, one after the other, there would be a definite difference to the sound quality, or texture, even though they are all playing the same thing.

Taking this example to the next stage, let's consider the pipes of a church organ. They range from being extremely small and thin to being thick and column-like. The small pipes produce the thin textured high notes and the thick pipes produce the deep resonant low notes. The texture of the sound will also alter depending on the materials the pipes are constructed from and their positioning within a room or space. We need to consider these basic principles when determining how to create different textures for our singing voice.

To create a warm, deep, resonant sound with our voice we need to alter the physical attributes of our instrument. Don't worry this does not involve any kind of surgery or long-term exercise regime. We simply alter the space in our body to emulate the large pipes of a church organ. Let's start by learning how to achieve these physical changes within ourselves.

# Exercise One

Throughout the exercises in this chapter, it is important to remain relaxed and comfortable. If you feel any strain or discomfort in your throat or any other part of your body, please stop practising and return to the exercises only when you are in a relaxed, comfortable state.

Practise singing a relatively low, but comfortable note to the sound of 'argh'. Ensure that the sound is free from any breathiness, as this will tire the voice quickly and alter your perception of the sound. Only continue with this exercise once you are happy with the quality of your sound. Stop singing and open your mouth, allowing yourself to yawn. As you yawn, feel what is happening to the tongue, back of your throat, mouth and neck. There are many reasons why we yawn, but the main purpose is to take in a large volume of oxygen. As such, the space in our mouth and throat expands to allow us to take in as much oxygen as possible. This expansion has created a 'bigger organ pipe' within us and any sound that is allowed to resonate in this space will have a deeper, more resonant quality. Attempt to speak whilst yawning and you will find that your sound quality alters dramatically.

Now practise creating the same expansion without yawning and then sing your practised 'argh' sound again. It is the same note, yet it sounds somehow deeper and warmer. If you put your hand flat against the top of your chest, you should also experience lots of vibration in the chest cavity.

**KEY POINTS**

* be relaxed and comfortable throughout

* practise singing a low 'argh' sound

* experience the physical changes that occur when yawning

* repeat the 'argh' sound whilst recreating the yawn space

* feel how the sound affects the chest cavity

Implementing the yawn technique will at first feel very strange and unnatural. Until now, you have probably never held a conversation or sung in this way. As with almost all the techniques in this book, allow yourself time to understand and develop the technique.

## Exercise Two

We are now going to make use of this new sound within part of a song. It is important that you either choose a song which is relatively low in pitch or that you alter your approach and sing the lyrics much lower than you usually would. Staying in the yawn position for an extended length of time can cause some discomfort, so please monitor yourself carefully and take a break where appropriate. Select one line or phrase only from your song and sing it without yawning until you feel comfortable with the low pitch and mouth shapes. Remind yourself of the yawn position and attempt the line again. If your line becomes obscured by the yawn, remember to over-exaggerate the mouth shape to compensate. Now practise the technique with different lines until you become confident with the technique.

### KEY POINTS

* choose a line from a song of your choice

* practise singing the line in a comfortable, low pitch

* apply the yawn technique to the line

* use mouth shapes to improve the clarity

* experiment with other lines

By this point, you should be confident that you can achieve a yawn sound. Just as you learned to pick and mix your mouth shape options in the previous chapter, you are now going to mix this technique with your natural sound. This will further highlight the benefits of the technique and allow you to have a more subtle approach to implementing this strange new sound.

# Exercise Three

When initially practising this exercise, it is advisable to slow down the lines of the song. This will allow you time to physically prepare for the techniques. Within a very short space of time, the switch will become much easier and you will be able to resume at normal speed.

Select a small section of the song that has four lines or phrases. You will be applying the yawn technique only to the first word of every line. The remainder of the line should be sung in your relaxed natural voice. If you are finding that the second word is also affected by the yawn, due to the switch of technique, then your delivery should be slowed even more. Practise until there is a smooth transition between techniques at the normal speed.

**KEY POINTS**

* select four lines from a song of your choice

* slow down the delivery of the song

* apply the yawn technique to the first word of each line

* ensure the yawn does not extend into the second word of the line

* repeat until there is a smooth transition at the normal speed

The yawn technique is making use of the chest resonating cavity. You should now be able to feel the vibration in your chest without using your hand as a guide.

If you are able to do this, then you have successfully developed your understanding and use of the CHEST VOICE.

For many years, the Chest Voice has been described as a tool that is only appropriate for lower notes. Using the yawn technique to create a 'bigger pipe', we can now carry some of the warm chest cavity characteristics through to the higher register of the voice.

This provides us with yet another sound effect to blend into our performances. The following exercise will guide you through attempting this safely. Please ensure that you are free from strain or struggle throughout.

## Exercise Four

Stand in a relaxed position with your feet shoulder width apart. Sing a relatively low but comfortable note to the sound of 'um'. When you reach the 'm' sound of 'um', your mouth should be closed and the sound will naturally become a hum. Practise this a few times until you are comfortable with the sound. Due to the low pitch and the resulting hum, this sound should feel relaxing and calming. When you get into the hum, smoothly slide the pitch of your voice upward with minimal effort. The upward slide in pitch should be slow and gradual, similar to the sound of a car engine slowly gathering speed. (IMPORTANT: Your chin should be very slightly lowered throughout. It is tempting to raise your head along with the rise in pitch. This creates tension around the larynx and may result in discomfort).

You will probably experience your sound cutting out as you reach the higher end of your voice. This is caused by a combination of tension on the larynx and incorrect airflow. You can work on this problem by leaning forward so your body becomes close to a right-angle shape. This allows the larynx to shift position due to gravity and you will find that you can reach higher notes in a more relaxed way. With time and practice, you will not need to lean forward to achieve the same result. Repeat the entire exercise whilst implementing the yawn Chest Voice technique.

**KEY POINTS**

* stand in a relaxed position

* sing a low note to the sound of 'um'

* allow the sound to become a hum

* slide the pitch of the sound slowly upward

* repeat the exercise, implementing the yawn Chest Voice technique

A good vocal performance combines correct pitching, timing, and a blend of textures. If you perform a song in the same way from beginning to end, the resulting sound can become boring and uninspiring. Making use of the chest voice will create a strong, thick foundation sound. On its own, this sound can be soulful but combined with other textures is amazing.

The Chest Voice is also easily practised at low volume which means that you can practise almost anywhere without disturbing others. It is great for warming up the voice before a performance. The low soothing tones vibrate through the larynx, which helps prepare the voice. It can also assist the recovery of a tired voice.

Experiment often with the Chest Voice so that you are comfortable enough to utilise it whenever required. As with all techniques, if you start to use the Chest Voice naturally in your performance then you are truly beginning to master it.

# Chapter completion checklist

Keep returning to the exercises in this chapter throughout your vocal development. You have successfully completed this chapter if you can agree with all of the statements below.

✓ I understand that singing 'soulfully' utilises the chest cavity

✓ I feel vibration occur in my chest

✓ I understand the term texture

✓ I know that deeper, warmer sounds come from a larger space than high sounds

✓ I understand the concept of yawning to alter my physical resonance space

✓ I can deliver a line of a song using the yawn technique

✓ I can switch the yawn technique on and off

✓ I can utilise the yawn technique with high notes

✓ I understand that combination of texture provides a more interesting performance than a single texture

# YOUR NOTES

# YOUR NOTES

# Chapter Nine

# Power Surge

Almost every singer that I work with asks for help increasing his or her vocal power. Power means the ability to project the voice loudly. One approach to achieving this goal is to practise being loud more often. This approach may work over an extended period, as it eventually strengthens the vocal muscles, but the risks involved in this approach seriously outweigh the benefits. I strongly advise against this. Prolonged loudness without proper control will lead to throat problems, which may include vocal nodes, lack of vocal stamina, hoarseness, an eventual reduction in the ability to perform clear high notes, and an end to a vocal career. There are many voice problems caused by pushing too hard.

During this chapter, we will be looking at ways to increase power, and perceived power, without the risks of damage to the voice. It is however, imperative, that you closely monitor your voice to ensure the exercises are being done correctly without stress, strain or pain.

In the previous chapter, we looked at the physical properties of a warm, deep sound for the purposes of introducing chest cavity technique. It is now important to understand the properties and concepts of creating powerful sound. The first and most obvious perceived property of power is singing at a louder volume. Higher volume is often achieved by physically exerting more energy and pushing air faster and harder across the larynx. Through doing this, you will quickly experience lots of the voice problems mentioned earlier.

We will be looking at alternative ways to increase volume. Think back to the church pipe organ example from the previous chapter. The pipes are big for low sound and small for high sound yet the overall volume of each note is the same. This proves that we actually need to use a very small amount of air to achieve a loud, high sound.

Let's start this series of different approaches to power with an exercise to develop the HEAD VOICE.

Powerful singing can be achieved without stressing the voice. The HEAD RESONATING CAVITY can help us achieve safe power. It may be worth revisiting the introduction to the head cavity that was outlined in the 'Vibration Station' chapter.

## Exercise One

Stand in a relaxed position and familiarise yourself with performing a head sound as outlined in Chapter Six. As you create this high, loud sound you should remain relaxed and feel no strain around the throat and neck. Look at yourself in a mirror to ensure that your neck does not look at all stressed or tensed. Once you are comfortable with your sound, hold it for longer, whilst gradually reducing the volume. Your aim is to maintain a pure, high-rounded sound without needing to force any part of your body. As your practice develops, you will notice that the sound remains strong and piercing even at low volume.

Once you can achieve this effortless strong sound, repeat the process in the following way. Take a full amount of air into your lungs and then gently breathe out half of the air again before starting the head sound. This may take a little practice as it can sometimes feel awkward starting a note without a full intake of air. This is because we have been conditioned throughout life to take a big breath before doing almost anything. This practice will help you trust your airflow more and realise just how little air is actually required to create a strong sound.

**KEY POINTS**
 * stand upright

 * sing a relaxed head sound as outlined in Chapter Six

 * hold the sound whilst gradually reducing the volume

 * practise achieving a strong, piercing sound at low volume

✴ repeat with a reduced initial intake of air

Exercise One has allowed you to experience a powerful sound at relatively low volume. The head voice is capable of achieving the pure rounded tones that can boost the power impact of any performance. Let's develop this technique further.

# Exercise Two

We will now be experimenting with keeping a pure head sound whilst singing other vowel sounds. Due to the natural shaping of various other vowels, it is important to monitor the best mouth shape for 'oi' and try to emulate this for other sounds. Start by singing a pure, high head tone sound with 'oi' and gradually step the pitch down five times smoothly, without a break in the sound. When you have sung the fifth note, take a breath and then smoothly climb back up through the pitches again until you are back at your original pitch. This will require lots of practice to achieve the pure head tone throughout. Although we a starting with 'oi' for every pitch it may still be necessary to alter mouth shape very slightly to achieve the best results. Practise this exercise with every vowel sound. Once you are happy that you are creating a strong head sound with every vowel, begin to mix and match the vowels sounds e.g. Lower the pitch with 'oi-o-e-a-e' and raise the pitch with 'e-a-e-o-oi'.

Refer back to the 'Vocal Effects Unit' chapter if you need to recap vowel sounds.

**KEY POINTS**

✴ sing a pure head tone sound to 'oi'

✴ gradually and smoothly step the pitch down five times without breaking the sound

✴ take a breath

✴ gradually and smoothly step the pitch up five times witout breaking the sound until you reach your original note

* repeat, replacing 'oi' with vowel sounds

* repeat, mixing and matching vowel sounds

Let's now learn to utilise the head voice alongside our natural voice. You should be able to switch between techniques smoothly and without any overspill into other words or syllables. The following exercise provides an opportunity for you to take a creative approach to singing. You will be provided with a line of lyrics to work with and no guidance on how the lyrics should be pitched, timed and performed. When working with a song you already know, it is tempting to try to recreate the sound of the performer. If you do not emulate the original sound closely enough, then the performance can sound wrong to your ears even though you may be giving an excellent performance in a different way. For this reason, the freedom of working with something new and unheard will allow you to concentrate on your sound and style, rather than that of another performer.

## Exercise Three

Whilst working with this exercise, you will be creating a strong, pure head sound on the first word of a line of lyrics. The remainder of the line can be sung in your natural voice or even mixed with a soulful sound. Do not be concerned with creating a beautiful melody worthy of a No.1 hit song, just ensure that the line can be sung comfortably in the way you choose. The lyrics to practise with are:

'Don't say goodbye'

Remember that while the word 'don't' should be sung as a comfortably high head tone, the rest is up to you. Ensure that your head tone does not carry through to the next word and that the transition of technique is smooth. This will take time, but will be worth the effort. Once you are happy with the results, why not create some lyrics of your own or sing sentences taken from any book. Sing lines with different vowel sounds at the start so that you can experiment fully with this technique.

**KEY POINTS**

    ✸  create a simple melody for the lyrics provided

    ✸  ensure the first word is a head tone

    ✸  practise the transition of technique

    ✸  experiment with other lyrics

You are now going to learn how to strengthen your inner larynx muscles. These control the action of the vocal cords (your vocal cords are not muscle). Our approach to this is via a speech level mechanism. You will be developing your strength and power via your spoken voice. Using this approach, we can safely deliver power notes with less breath and pressure, whilst developing the inner larynx muscles.

# Exercise Four

During this exercise, we will again be working on a small section of a song that you will choose. Power is not range (i.e. how high or low you are able to sing) so ensure that your chosen song is within your current capabilities. You will improve your range during the chapter 'Sing Higher And Lower Than Ever Before'. Start by clapping the rhythm of the vocal part to establish where each syllable is. If you are unsure how to do this, then you should refer back to 'Get With The Beat'. Now sing the melody replacing every syllable with the sound 'gug', e.g. 'you left me all alone' would become 'Gug gug gug gug gug-gug'. The gug should be sung toward the mouth and nose area, which simply involves raising your cheeks with a smile and lifting your nose very slightly.

Now practise the section of the song without pushing the voice hard. Pushing too hard will create unwanted tension in or around the throat area. The 'gug' sound not only helps reduce breath during sound, but also allows the vocal cords to position correctly. Try to make this exercise a five-minute part of your daily singing practice and notice how easy singing becomes in just two weeks.

## KEY POINTS

* ✳ choose a small section from a song

* ✳ ensure the range is within current capabilities

* ✳ clap the rhythm of the vocal part to identify syllables

* ✳ sing the section replacing every syllable with 'gug'

* ✳ notice how 'gug' reduces air over sound

One of the major factors when considering power singing is that it can be perceived in so many different ways. The performer may feel that they are not giving enough to a performance just because they are not sweaty, tense and tired at the end. I hope that by this stage you understand that this view of power is not a professional one. Audiences recognise and determine power by experiencing intensity and volume. During the next part of this chapter, we are going to discover how to use our audience's perception to our advantage.

I'm sure that you can think of a song that starts very quietly with few instruments and then suddenly bursts into a loud, upbeat, full sound. Many songs use drums to create a sudden new level of excitement. This dynamic change gives the audience an impression of intensity and power.

We can easily utilise a similar approach with our voice. A sudden or gradual alteration of volume will create a better experience of power for any audience. If we feel that we cannot give part of a song enough power, we simply reduce the volume of other parts of the song to ensure dramatic and dynamic change occurs. With microphone technology readily available, it is possible to sing at extremely low volume, and still be heard. This provides us with great opportunity to make our 'not-quite-loud-enough' sound seem 'amazingly loud'. Practise altering the volume levels of your performances to utilise this approach and discover the power that you already have.

# Chapter completion checklist

Keep returning to the exercises in this chapter throughout your vocal development. You have successfully completed this chapter if you can agree with all of the statements below.

✓ I understand that power is the ability to project the voice clearly

✓ I understand the risks of incorrect practice

✓ I practise power without stress, strain or pain

✓ I can create effortless 'loud' sounds on every vowel sound using the head voice

✓ I can blend the head voice technique into a performance

✓ I am practising every day to strengthen and develop my inner larynx muscles

✓ I understand the concept of power perception from an audience's point of view

# YOUR NOTES

# YOUR NOTES

# YOUR NOTES

Chapter Ten

# Sing Higher And Lower
# Than Ever Before

Many singers and voice coaches develop the range (how high or low we can sing) of a performer by steadily pushing the voice to its extremes. This usually involves singing high and low notes in practice sessions until either the right notes are achieved or the performer is exhausted and hoarse. This is an extremely hit-and-miss approach to voice development and can very often end up shrinking a range due to the damage caused. During this chapter, you will learn to increase your range in an effortless way, concentrating on making what you are able to achieve now so comfortable, that expanding the range becomes easy. Exercises in this chapter will enable you to start increasing your range by many notes within a very short space of time.

Singing higher and lower notes than ever before involves improved control of the vocal cords through developing the inner muscles of the larynx. Air initially opens and activates the sound produced by our vocal cords, but too much will cause the cords to vibrate too far apart causing a very limited upper range.

In order to understand how the vocal cords work, place your hands flat together in front of you. From this prayer-like position, keep fingertips and the bottom of your palms together whilst bending both hands into right angles. You should now have a diamond shape between your hands. Closing your hands almost together again represents the required shape for the vocal cords to produce a high note and as the diamond becomes bigger, the note produced will become lower. Once again, consider the church pipe organ example to highlight that a small opening, or pipe, will produce a higher sound than a big opening. Too much airflow will force this opening to be bigger.

It is a myth that in order to reach a high note, you should get loud and push the voice. This will only demonstrate that your voice is out of control and you are counting on luck to make the right sound happen. If you are unable to sing a sound at low volume, then you should not even be attempting to sing it at loud volume.

The following exercises work by training your inner larynx muscles to respond correctly to pitches that are comfortable to you at a speech level. Once this is mastered, you will find that your range expands without even trying. I am not suggesting that this technique will allow your range to expand by only a couple of notes. Results should be noticeable within a few weeks and in some cases, you may find that your range expands by over twelve notes! This process is not only much safer than other range-expanding techniques; it is also much faster.

## Exercise One

Let's begin by understanding where our current safe range is. To help you relax, you may sit down when working on this exercise. Start by voicing an easy, short, medium pitched note to 'la'. Gradually step up to higher pitches, taking a breath wherever required and keep your head in the same relaxed position. As you step up through the pitches, do not exert any more effort than you would if you were speaking. Remember, you are finding your safe pitches and not trying to prove anything. When you reach your maximum safe pitch at low volume, your voice will either cut off the sound, change in texture or suddenly shift into an extremely high, false sound. Whatever you experience, you will instinctively know when you are no longer able to EFFORTLESSLY raise the pitch of your voice. Repeat the exercise again, this time taking the pitch slowly and gradually down instead of up.

**KEY POINTS**
* sit in a relaxed upright position

* sing a medium pitched note to 'la' at speech level

* gradually step up through higher notes, ensuring you remain at speech level

* stop when you can no longer raise the pitch in an effortless way

* repeat the exercise this time taking the pitch down instead of up

During exercise one, you may have felt that what you were able to achieve was not a true representation of your range and indeed this is case. The notes you were able to sing comfortably are the notes that you will be initially working with. The exercise was also designed to allow you to feel how to sing in your safe range. This range will rapidly expand and you may even find that you can stay comfortable at higher pitches as we work with the next exercise. Won't it be wonderful when notes that are currently out of your range become that easy to sing?

This is where the silly sounds begin. As you progress through the next exercises, you will be asked to repeat the gradually raising and lowering pitch exercise with other sounds. The sounds given are designed to work the inner larynx muscles in a particular way and all have a specific, targeted action on the muscles.

## Exercise Two

We have already discovered that too much air will literally blow the vocal cords open and dramatically reduce overall range and control. This exercise is designed to help you effortlessly reduce the airflow whilst creating sound. You will repeat Exercise One using a different sound. This time replace 'la' with 'nay'. As you produce the sound, ensure that your cheeks are raised by adopting a wide grin. The grin should be over-exaggerated and this will create a little tension around the nose. The resulting sound will have a nasal quality. Do not worry about this being a strange sound as this is an exercise to develop the muscle, and is not a performance technique. 'Nay' is ideal sound to reduce air automatically so you do not have to worry about over-blowing.

You may have already noticed that it is quite difficult to produce the 'nay' sound in a breathy way. As you gradually raise and lower the pitch of your voice, ensure that you remain at speech level with an effortless approach. You may notice that 'nay' allows you to sing higher immediately. You obviously cannot perform songs singing 'nay' all the way through, so work daily with this exercise to prepare your muscles to operate correctly with other sounds too. You should practise with 'nay' for at least two weeks before moving on to Exercise Three.

**KEY POINTS**
* repeat Exercise One using the sound 'nay'

* stop when you can no longer raise the pitch in an effortless way

* repeat the exercise, this time taking the pitch down instead of up

Before attempting Exercise Three it is important to consider your progress so far. Do you feel that your safe range is more comfortable than before, or perhaps has expanded? If you feel that no real progress has occurred, it may be worth considering your approach to the exercises.

Imagine that you are just about to sing a high sound. As you prepare, you may find that you immediately create a slight tension at the back of your throat or neck. This is your body saying 'this note is going to be hard to sing'. If you approach any of these exercises with the same tense sensation, you are confirming your belief that high is difficult. It may be worth shrinking your safe range until your body is convinced that producing sound is effortless.

This tension, when preparing for a note, is a psychological block that you need to undo by closely monitoring your body's responses during practice. Tension and strain are never required to become a great singer.

# Exercise Three
Repeat the previous exercise replacing the sound with 'goog' (The 'oo' sound should be voiced as in Good not Moon). This sound gets to work on a different set of muscles and you may find that

your range is once again reduced slightly until you grow comfortable with the technique.

**KEY POINTS**

* repeat Exercise One using the sound 'goog'

* stop when you can no longer raise the pitch in an effortless way

* repeat the exercise, this time taking the pitch down instead of up

# Exercise Four

This time replace the sound with 'gug'. This exercises the muscles in a completely different way. You should practise until you are confident that the tones are relaxed and non-breathy.

**KEY POINTS**

* repeat Exercise One using the sound 'gug'

* stop when you can no longer raise the pitch in an effortless way

* repeat the exercise, this time taking the pitch down instead of up

# Exercise Five

By now, you will have worked with the non-breathy tones and should be confident that your control and range have improved to some extent. This exercise will now introduce three new sounds for your experimentation. The sounds carry a greater likelihood of over-blowing and require a higher degree of self-monitoring. Make sure that your tones are pure, free of strain and not breathy.

Repeat the technique learned in Exercise One and replace the sound with 'mar', 'may' and finally 'go'. As you progress through these sounds, pay special attention to the effect that the shape of your mouth is having on the sound. Your mouth is a resonating cavity and should position to form the right shapes, ensuring that your tones are both easier to achieve and have continuity.

**KEY POINTS**

* repeat Exercise One using the sounds
   'mar', 'may' and 'go'

* stop when you can no longer raise the pitch in an effortless way

* repeat the exercise, this time taking the pitch down instead of up

* pay particular attention to your airflow

* utilise mouth shapes to achieve best results

## Visualisation

To assist with focus, and develop a consistent approach, some voice students find it helpful to visualise the sound being directed in a particular way. Try the following exercise when practising higher sounds.

# Exercise Six

This exercise is based on a vocal technique called 'forward projection'. Forward projection involves aiming your voice at either imaginary or real targets. This kind of projection relies on your imagination to create a more open vocal style.

Imagine you are standing on a diving board or similar raised object. Lower your head slightly and visualise water or any other object several metres below you. You are about to create a sound which will be aimed at your imaginary object. Sing a note that is near the top of your safe range and visualise the object moving or vibrating because of the sound you make.

Once you are able to visualise this and are happy with the sound that you create, experiment with a variety of different sounds and mouth shapes.

**KEY POINTS**

- ✳ visualise standing on a raised platform

- ✳ imagine an object or surface far below you

- ✳ aim your 'safe' high sounds at the imaginary target

- ✳ experiment with a variety of shapes and sounds

## *Bridging the gap*

When you move between high and low sounds (or between reso-nating cavities), you may find that the transition between sections of your voice can be weak. These 'shifts' in the voice are often re-ferred to as BRIDGES. Many professional singers can hit high and low sounds with strength and character; there is, however, often a small section of the range that is in between these comfortable areas. This bridge needs to be developed.

During the next exercise, we will be increasing your range and practising a smooth transition between resonating cavities. Spend time on this exercise to understand the body's response to the sound and the subtle sensations that occur.

## Exercise Seven

This exercise involves sliding from low safe sounds to high safe sounds. Start by placing your hand on the top of your chest and singing a low 'argh' sound. You should utilise the chest cavity technique when starting this. As you repeat the sound, imagine a ball is spinning inside your chest where the vibration is occur-ring. Once you are happy with this sensation, slide the pitch of the notes gradually upward. This should be a sliding sound (i.e. like a car engine increasing speed) rather than stepping-up sound (i.e. a scale).

As you practise, imagine the spinning ball moving gently up through the resonating cavities. Starting in the chest, the ball should travel smoothly up the back of the neck, then into the mouth. It should finish its journey at the back of your head as you reach the high sounds (head resonance). Practise this exercise daily. Ensure no tension occurs and the passage of the voice between resonating areas is as smooth as possible. This exercise will improve your bridge, increase your range and heighten your awareness of resonation.

**KEY POINTS**

* perform a low chest resonating 'argh sound'

* slide the sound smoothly upward

* visualise a spinning ball that moves, with your voice, through the resonating cavities

During this chapter, you have learned safe ways to develop range by conditioning the inner larynx muscles. Ensure your practice of range work continues throughout your career to maintain and develop optimal sounds.

## Quick Tip

During previous rhythm exercises, we used the sound 'bib' to keep with the beat. Try practising any particularly high sections of a song with the 'bib' sound. As well as a great rhythm tool, it is a good, short, non-breathy sound and can quickly smooth out tension in high areas.

# Chapter completion checklist

Keep returning to the exercises in this chapter throughout your vocal development. You have successfully completed this chapter if you can agree with all of the statements below.

✓ I understand that regularly pushing the voice to extremes will cause damage and fatigue

✓ I understand that the safest way to expand the range is by gently conditioning the inner larynx muscles

✓ I experience no tension or strain when I work through the exercises in this chapter

✓ I understand what is meant by the term bridge

✓ I have noticed that my safe range has expanded

# YOUR NOTES

# Chapter Eleven

# Keeping It Real

The most important part of any performance is the artist's ability to engage an audience. An audience wants to have some kind of emotional experience from what they see and hear. After all, that is why they bought the ticket! It is not enough just to sing the right notes in the right order if you want to create attention. During this chapter we will investigate what audiences react to, and develop a method for ensuring our vocal delivery is emotionally 'real' and does not disappoint the audience.

First, it is important to understand a little about how the human brain works. Don't worry, you don't need a psychology degree to understand these basic concepts!

Our brain can be divided into two parts. The first part is often referred to as the 'old brain' and is positioned toward the rear of our skull. This section of the brain is called 'old' because it was the first part of the brain to evolve. The 'old brain' deals with emotion and is not particularly rational.

The second section is called the 'new brain'. This part evolved later. It is positioned toward the front of the skull. The 'new brain' deals with our rational thoughts and logical intelligence. To take an audience on an emotional experience, we need to stimulate the 'old brain'.

To put this into perspective let's take the simple example of a shopping trip. When we see a perfect outfit or some other attractive item, our 'old brain' always reacts first by giving us an emotion, then the 'new brain' kicks in with logic and we question our emotion with comments including "do I really need it?" or "can I afford it?". If our emotion is strong enough then impulse buying occurs and we can often regret our purchase later. Many salespeople are taught that every human reacts to emotion first and intelligence second. This is why adverts tend to be geared toward creating emotion rather than presenting bland facts.

To trigger the emotion of our audience, first we have to convey basic human emotion in our performance. For centuries it has been understood that HOW we speak generates more of a message than the words themselves. Anyone who has ever misinterpreted a text message will understand this principle. So what is the best way to convey the right emotional stimuli in a song?

The first step is to develop an understanding of the song's intended message. Obviously we can look at lyrical meaning, but it is also important to understand the emotion conveyed in the music itself. We can add to this with our vocal style. Lyrics alone are not enough to deliver the message.

## Exercise One

During this exercise we will be practising in order to value and understand the powerful messages hidden within the music. You will not require any lyrics for this section. It is important that you approach this work with an open mind. Prepare to be surprised by emotions that perhaps conflict with how you perceive the lyrics.

Find a time and place to practise where you will not be disturbed. Sit or lie down comfortably and get yourself into a relaxed state. The breathing exercises learned earlier in the book may help you into relaxation. Play the backing track for your chosen song and listen to the overall sounds. Ask yourself what the music is suggesting. What images do you see in your mind whilst listening, and how do you feel? The images in your mind do not need to make sense, but will help you to develop a heightened sense of emotion.

Listen to the music several times. Write down some keywords that describe your listening experience. It is important to stress that these keywords should not be based on what you already know about the song. Keywords should be based on what you feel from the music alone. Often the saddest love songs can be set to wonderful uplifting and inspiring music that contrasts entirely to the lyrical content.

Consider how your vocal approach could blend with, and highlight, the musical message. This will enable you to deliver a unique and powerful performance.

**KEY POINTS**

* find a quiet relaxing practice environment

* listen to the music only of your chosen song

* allow the music to guide your imagination and evoke emotion

* write down key words that describe your listening experience

* use this information to create a unique emotional delivery

Now that you have a deeper awareness of the musical content, we can spend time understanding the lyrics. The first step is to understand the flow of the story. Lyrics can be as clear as a written story but can, on occasion, make no sense at all to anyone but the writer. Whatever the content of your chosen song, it will have a beginning, an end and should represent a journey. Imagine travelling along in a car to get to your destination. On your journey, you may look out of the window and see all kinds of wonderful, interesting things. In your song's journey, it is your responsibility to create as many points of interest along the way. Techniques for this will be explained later in the chapter. Let's take some time now to address the interpretation of lyrical content.

# Exercise Two

Read the entire lyrics of your song and summarise the story by writing keywords or a very short paragraph of text. Now read the lyrics again and imagine an alternative story that is still relevant to the lyrics. Often you will find that lyrics are written quite loosely in order that the audience can create their own story. Your task is to find a story within the lyrics that YOU believe in.

Your performance MUST reflect your interpretation because, for the duration of the performance, the audience needs to believe that the song is owned by you. As you imagine your own story for the lyrics, try to see, hear and feel every aspect in your mind. This will help create the emotions within you.

**KEY POINTS**

* read the lyrics

* summarise the story

* find alternative stories that may also fit

* choose a story and allow yourself to explore the emotions within it

In order to keep the emotion real in the song, it is useful to look at the comparisons between singing and speech. If we understand how emotion is conveyed in speech, then we can use this in our singing to create real audience belief. This is just like acting. This skill will make your performance real and not just an attempt at recreating the emotions of the original artist. If you do not feel real emotion in your performance, then your audience has no chance of feeling emotion.

Pace, inflection and dynamics are all involved in conveying emotion in speech and we can utilise these tools to give vocal performances better impact. The following sections describe these tools in further detail.

## *Pace*

Pace is the speed of delivery. Many performers believe that this cannot be altered during a performance, because a vocalist needs to follow the speed of the backing music. Although this is true to some extent, we can still alter the PERCEIVED speed of our delivery. The following exercise demonstrates three tricks to affect perceived pace.

# Exercise Three

N.B If possible, use a recording device during the following exercise so that you can hear the results of pace alteration.

Choose a line from a song of your choice. Sing the line normally to familiarise yourself with the natural flow of the melody. Now repeat the line singing smoothly and joining each word to each other (i.e. with no gaps at all between the notes). This makes the melody flow and gives the effect of a slower pace. Now try the opposite of this by making each note short, detached and punchy. This gives the melody more urgency and gives the illusion that it is faster. The third trick involves altering the start point of each line. Experiment with singing the lines slightly before and after where they are supposed to be. You will only be able to adjust your timing very slightly without it sounding wrong. This slight timing adjustment can add a 'laid-back' or 'urgent' element to your vocal style.

## KEY POINTS

* choose a line from any song

* sing the line normally to familiarise yourself

* sing the line smoothly joining each note together (SLOW)

* sing the notes of the line short and detached (FAST)

* experiment with the effect of timing alteration

## *Inflections*

Inflections are changes in pitch of the spoken voice to create meaning and emphasis (as explained in the chapter 'Where's My Voice'). Whilst singing, the melody controls the pitch of the message. In order to highlight the inflections of our song, we must compare the meaning of the lyrics to the relative pitch of the melody.

# Exercise Four

Think back to the inflection exercise we covered in the chapter 'Where's My Voice'. We took our speech inflection to a level where it emulated the musical pitch of a song. This exercise will reverse this process to find the real meaning of the musical inflection. You will need some paper and a pen or pencil for this exercise.

Draw a horizontal line on your paper. This line will represent a mid-range pitch over time. Now look at the first line of your song. Draw a rough curved line through your horizontal line which represents the melody (i.e. high notes would take your line above the horizontal and low notes would curve below etc.) You should now have a basic graphical representation of your melody that will help you understand the inflections within it.

Now speak the line and try to follow the same inflection pattern as your curved line. Do not try to copy the melody exactly with your speech; just ensure that you inflect in a similar way. Notice how this inflection gives particular meaning to the line. This has highlighted how the melody is steering the perceived meaning of the song. Now you have the basic principle of melodic inflection, look at other lines in the song to discover what they are actually conveying.

## KEY POINTS

* draw a curved line that represents the pitch in your melody

* transfer the basic pitch changes into speech inflection

* notice how this natural inflection gives meaning to the line

* repeat with other lines in your song

## *Dynamics*

Dynamics describes the effect of soft and loud volumes. During the chapter 'Power Surge', we experimented with the effect of dynamics on perceived power. Shifting dynamics within each line creates a much more stimulating sound for the audience. Dynamics are one of the most underestimated tools in music. Great performers like Aretha Franklin, Celine Dion, Barbara Streisand and Stevie Wonder have perfected the art of dynamics to such an extent that they often change the dynamics from syllable to syllable. Most amateur singers will sing a verse softly and perhaps give a chorus more volume to display their awareness of dynamics. This works reasonably well, but still makes an audience endure large sections of the song with no dynamic change. During the next exercise, you will learn to bring each word of a song to life with smooth dynamics.

# Exercise Five

Sing any comfortable note to the sound of 'oh'. Hold the note for several seconds. Repeat this note at a quieter volume and slowly increase then decrease the volume. Concentrate on keeping the note clear, with a good sound quality. You may need to practise this over a few days to get the desired quality. Once you have achieved a good control over the volume, sing the whole song. As you sing the song, take the volume from loud to soft every few seconds. This will create a regular pulse of dynamics.

The resulting song will be unsuitable for performance but is training you to take charge of dynamics. When you can achieve a good dynamic pulse, sing the song again and position your dynamics strategically to create a continually dynamic and 'real' performance. As you progress through this exercise, you will experience a feeling of added control over the entire performance.

**KEY POINTS**

* practise dynamic change on one note

* ensure your note remains clear and is a good quality tone

* sing the entire song creating a dynamic pulse throughout

* repeat the song carefully placing the dynamics strategically for a 'real' performance

By now, you should have a good understanding of how emotional representation can have a massive effect on your audience's perception. You will now also be feeling a higher degree of control over your sound.

## Chapter completion checklist

Keep returning to the exercises in this chapter throughout your vocal development. You have successfully completed this chapter if you can agree with all of the statements below.

✓ I understand that an audience reacts to performance on an emotional level

✓ I understand the reasons for the emotional response

✓ I understand that speech techniques offer ways to represent a song emotionally

✓ I can effectively control a dynamic delivery

✓ I have noticed that I now have increased vocal control

# YOUR NOTES

# Chapter Twelve

# Advanced Effects

During this chapter, you will be practising some advanced vocal concepts. Before attempting any of the exercises in the chapter, it is important that you have successfully completed all of the previous work and have fully understood all of the principles set out so far.

## *The Soft Palette*

The first advanced tool we will be practising with is the implementation of palette placement. The soft palette is a vital tool for filtering the sound at the final stage of resonating cavity production. You can locate the soft palette by placing your thumb gently on the roof of the mouth. You will then be feeling a hard surface near the front of your mouth (hard palette). Now slide your thumb slowly backwards and you will feel the surface become softer; this is the soft palette. The soft palette consists of muscular fibres. It has been in action throughout all the previous chapters of this book. We will now learn to heighten our awareness of the soft palette and control the subtle filtering of sound.

## Exercise One

This exercise is a basic introduction to placement and will help you to understand how sound is filtered by the soft palette depending on the type of sound being produced. Start by saying the word 'sing'. You will notice that the back of the tongue touches the soft palette during the 'ng' part of the word. This action closes off a lot of the natural mouth resonance and directs the sound to your nose. Now say the word 'ink'. You will feel an opening and closing sensation at the back of your mouth. This sensation is the soft palette

shaping the resonation whilst holding back and then releasing the airflow. To demonstrate further how the soft palette can control air release, say the sound 'k'. Notice how your breath is held back and then released to produce the sound. Experiment with other sounds to understand the action of the soft palette.

**KEY POINTS**

  * know where the soft palette is

  * say an 'ng' sound and notice the filtering to the nose

  * say 'ink' and notice the opening and closing sensation

  * say 'k' to feel the control of breath

  * experiment with other sounds to see how the soft palette filters

Now that you have experienced some of the effect and control of the soft palette, we will concentrate on using this muscle to aim our sound when singing. The following exercise will allow you to experience the difference in tonal quality when we filter sound into different spaces in our mouth.

## Exercise Two

Start by positioning the tongue and soft palette in the 'ng' position. The tongue should be raised at the back and touching the soft palette. We are now going to produce a small whining sound. This sound will be similar to that of a whining puppy. Very little air is needed to produce this sound. Move the pitch of the sound around slightly until you become very comfortable with the sensation and the quality of tone produced. When you are comfortable with, and in control of this sound, move the sound around your mouth in a figure of eight pattern (i.e. the figure of eight

should be entirely in your mouth. One side of the eight should touch the roof of your mouth and the other side should touch your tongue. The top of the eight should be by your lips and the bottom should be at the back of your throat. The crossover of the figure eight pattern should occur slightly above the centre of your tongue.

To help visualise this pattern position, imagine that you could squash the spaces within the eight by bringing the roof of your mouth and tongue together). Notice how the quality of sound alters as it resonates in different areas of your mouth. Experiment with the whole of your vocal range using this figure of eight technique.

**KEY POINTS**

* start in the 'ng' position

* create a small whining sound

* get comfortable with this sound across different pitches

* move the sound around in a figure of eight shape

* notice the sound quality change within the shape

* experiment with your entire range using the figure of eight technique

## *Lip Rolling*

The term 'Lip Rolling' describes a technique for safely working the entire muscle range and smoothing out transitions between resonating areas (Bridges). This technique is a personal favourite of mine as it allows me to gain additional control through better airflow, reduce the level of effort, and rapidly expand my range. This technique will yield surprising results within just two weeks if practised for at least ten minutes daily. Lip rolling is sometimes referred to as 'bubbling' and some voice coaches have based entire singing programmes on this technique.

The following exercises will allow you to experience this basic technique whilst applying your entire range to the practice.

# Exercise One

The initial lip rolling technique can sometimes take a little practice. It is imperative that the basic technique is mastered before moving on to Exercise Two. Close your mouth with your teeth loosely together and your cheeks raised slightly into a half smile. Your lips should be together and pouted so they are sticking out but loose and relaxed. Inhale through your nose and gently push the air out through your lips. The air pressure should push breath past your lips causing them to rapidly 'flap' and create an engine type noise. It is important to allow your lips to be as relaxed as possible so that the air can cause maximum movement. Do not push the air too hard. Make this process as relaxed as possible. Practise this process until you can create the 'lip rolling' with minimal exertion. You may find that this exercise causes a tickling sensation in your nose – this is quite normal.

**KEY POINTS**
- ✳ close your mouth with teeth loosely together and your cheeks raised slightly with a half-smile

- ✳ pout your lips loosely

- ✳ inhale through the nose

- ✳ push air out through the mouth causing the lips to move rapidly through air pressure alone

After becoming comfortable with this basic technique, you will now be able to combine this with sound. The mechanics of this exercise ensure that correct airflow and muscle control are maintained. If you are not correctly engaging correct air or muscle control, you will notice that this basic technique breaks down and the lip movement stops involuntarily. This makes the exercise ideal for self-monitoring.

# Exercise Two
Recreate the lip rolling from the previous exercise. At the same time as the basic lip rolling, create a sound. The sound should be relaxed and not pushed too hard. With the lips still rolling, slide your sound up and down in pitch. Practise this until you are happy that you have a wide range of relaxed pitch movement.

After you have mastered pitch sliding, try to step up and down through individual notes like a scale. The idea of the exercise is to apply your entire safe range whilst lip rolling. Have patience, it may take several attempts to achieve the correct approach. If you have difficulty in reaching higher sounds or you are experiencing some tension, try bending forward. This allows the larynx to hang in a more relaxed, lower position rather than being jerked upward with tension. After daily practice, (for at least two weeks), you will notice that your general singing style becomes more relaxed and controlled.

**KEY POINTS**
* recreate lip rolling

* apply a sound to the lip roll

* slide your sound up and down through various pitches

* step notes up and down through your safe range

## *Breathy Tones*

Breathy tones can be used to great effect in singing, but it is imperative to apply the additional breath in a safe, controlled way. If too much air is produced with a sound, there is a risk of incorrect pitching or unstable control. This section looks at applying breath to a good tone rather than over-blowing whilst creating the tone. Breathy vocals are ideally suited to sad, romantic, sexy and intimate styles. The following exercises will allow you to achieve good practice in creating a breathy style.

# Exercise One

During this exercise, you will be creating a single sound and adding a breathy quality safely. Start by singing a mid-range sound to a 'mmm'. This sound should be like a hum and your soft palette will be directing the sound to the mouth and nose. As you practise this, change the sound from 'mmm' into a soft 'argh' sound. You should notice that the sound has developed a breathy quality without producing excess airflow. The shape of the mouth and the soft attack has allowed your voice to sound more breathy.

**KEY POINTS**
* sing a 'mmm' sound

* change the 'mmm' into a soft 'argh'

* notice the mouth shaping and sound attack

During the next exercise you will learn to apply this concept of breathiness into your song.

## Exercise Two

This exercise involves re-using the 'harsh air monitor' exercise learned in the chapter 'Vocal Effects Unit'. On this occasion, we will be using it for monitoring the control of breathy sounds. The idea of this exercise is to create a breathy sound without allowing airflow to interrupt the quality of the tone. Place your hand flat approximately two inches in front of your mouth and sing your song in a breathy style. You will feel air hitting your hand as you practise.

Adjust your mouth shapes and the level of air pressure to create a clear breathy sound without too much air hitting your hand. Practising this technique will not only improve your tonal quality, but will also improve your microphone technique when singing in this style.

**KEY POINTS**

* if necessary, revisit the chapter 'Vocal Effects Unit'

* place your hand flat approximately two inches in front of your mouth

* sing in a breathy style adjusting mouth shapes and air pressure to reduce air impact on your hand

### Falsetto

Falsetto means 'false voice' and describes the area of the voice that is outside the normal range of the singing voice. It can be recognised as the sound of the Bee Gees' or even the very high tone of a man impersonating a woman. Some classical voice teachers describe this as the 'head voice' although this sound is quite different from the head voice techniques in modern teachings (including this book).

Falsetto is not a necessary part of voice development, but can be used to good effect in some songs or as part of backing vocals. As the falsetto is an area of the voice that is rarely used, (because it is so unnatural in everyday speech), it usually requires a lot of practice to achieve a usable sound. There are two main approaches to a falsetto sound. Although both approaches generate the sound in the same way, the filtering process creates two very different sounds. The following exercise will take you through both approaches. As with all exercises, the falsetto practice should be free of tension, struggle and pain.

# Exercise One

You will first need to identify and produce a high sound outside of your usual range, this can usually be achieved by producing a 'whoo-hoo' type sound or perhaps revisit the soft palette whining exercise. Once you are able to produce this high sound, hold one high note only. Use the sound of 'or' and drop your jaw to fully open your mouth into a vertical position. Repeat this sound several times to get used to the sound and improve its clarity. Step the sound up and down through pitches. You will notice that your falsetto range is quite small in comparison to your normal range. You have now achieved the basic first approach to falsetto and this area should be practised daily to strengthen and develop it.

The second approach involves filtering this pure sound through the nose. Start with the basic 'or' sound and, whilst staying on the same note, change the sound into 'ung' and alter your mouth shape to a horizontal position (wide). You will notice the soft palette shift position and the sound becomes less pure and has some nasal qualities. Now you know where this sound is directed to, try going straight into it with a 'yang' sound. Keep your mouth shape horizontal as you do this. This second approach to falsetto is more similar to the Bee Gees' style than the first approach. Practise singing various lines of your favourite songs in the falsetto style.

**KEY POINTS**
   * sing a high (out of normal range) sound to 'or'

* open your mouth vertically and repeat until comfortable and relaxed

* change the sound from open 'or' to wide 'ung' and notice the quality of tone change

* sing a falsetto sound to 'yang' to achieve the nasal quality

* practise lines from various songs with both styles of falsetto

Now you have completed this chapter, you are armed with even more techniques to gain extra control and variation to your sound.

# Chapter completion checklist

Keep returning to the exercises in this chapter throughout your vocal development. You have successfully completed this chapter if you can agree with all of the statements below.

✓ I have mastered previous chapters before practising the techniques in this chapter

✓ I understand where the soft palette is and how it affects my sound

✓ I notice how my sound changes as I practise the figure of eight technique

✓ I understand the lip rolling technique and reasons for using it

✓ I have practised the lip rolling technique for more than two weeks and my singing has become easier and more controlled

✓ I understand the dangers of incorrect breathy tones

✓ I am able to monitor my airflow on breathy tones

✓ I understand the term falsetto and I am able to use both falsetto approaches

# YOUR NOTES

# YOUR NOTES

# YOUR NOTES

## Chapter Thirteen

# Rock Tricks

Rock vocals have evolved through a variety of styles over the years and the only true link between the styles has been the raw emotion and power. In the past I have worked with, and interviewed, many rock vocalists as well as personally spending years as a vocalist for a gigging rock band. One of the major things I have noticed is the desire not to conform to any traditional singing techniques, and to let high levels of volume and emotion reign supreme.

For some rock vocalists, a singing career can be very short lived due to the extremes to which the voice is pushed. Competing with huge guitar amps and singing or screaming without any kind of regard for vocal health will almost certainly cause major voice problems and even vocal nodes. Nodes can alter and limit a voice forever. In this chapter we will be looking at techniques for creating rock sounds and learning how to perform them safely.

Please be aware that this chapter comes after the majority of other voice work. It is important that you have a good understanding of voice techniques from previous chapters and that you practise the following exercises within your own safe capabilities. Offer me a list of rock vocalists who have enjoyed a long career, and I'll offer you a list of techniques and voice coaches that they have worked with. If you are serious about your music, you need to be serious about your voice. This doesn't mean you will end up sounding like an operatic old granny; it means you will have a deeper understanding of your art, and develop vocal power to be proud of.

Each technique offered in this chapter can be used individually or combined to create a quality rock tone that is unique to you. Don't forget to also practise the power and range techniques from previous chapters.

### Vocal Attack

When you listen to fast-paced rock music, you notice the energy and the apparent anger, or other raw emotions, of the music. There are generally more punchy sounds than smooth sounds. Listen to various pieces of rock music and pay particular attention to the bass and drums. These two elements of the music are the foundation for everything else and provide the overall drive of the music. Listen to how all of the instruments fit in with each other and how space between notes is used to create more tension. One of the most popular rock techniques is 'fast attack'. This literally means that the volume of what you sing is higher, and the note length is shorter, at chosen points within the rhythmical framework of the music. The following exercise outlines how to add this attack to your vocal.

# Exercise One

To achieve a fast vocal attack you must think of your voice as a percussive instrument. When you listen to a drum sound you will notice that the sound is loud immediately, has very little length and has a definite end, rather than a fade out. Think back to the rhythm exercises in the chapter 'Get With The Beat'. We used the sound 'bib' to highlight the rhythm of the melody. This sound is fast and helps our rhythmic accuracy.

We are now going to shorten this sound further by replacing it with 'b' (pronounced 'ber' not 'bee'). We need to find the main beat of the music with the count 1,2,3,4. Some music will require the count to be to a different number, but most rock music uses the standard four count. Start by counting along with the main beat of the music (refer to the chapter 'Get With The Beat' if you are having difficulty finding the main beat). When you are happy with your count, replace the numbers with the short 'b' sound.

You are now highlighting the points in the music where your vocal needs to be loudest. Look at the lyrics and find which words or part-words fall on these main beats. Now sing your line making each note short and percussive and ensuring the main beat syllables are the loudest.

Experiment with your vocal attack in various other rhythmical patterns i.e. attack only on beats two and four, one and three or even between numbers on the off-beats. This technique adds impact and aggression to your vocal. It is best suited to fast rock but feel free to experiment with all styles of rock.

**KEY POINTS**

* think of your vocal as a percussive sound

* sing the main beats of the music with the sound 'b'

* find the words or part-words that fall on the main beat

* sing the line percussively ensuring that the main beats are loudest

* experiment with other 'attack' rhythmical patterns

* experiment with various styles of rock using this technique

Harsher sounds can be achieved by filtering the sound toward the nasal area. Guitars in rock music are often played through a distortion pedal that adds a harsh depth to the sound. You can also add a natural distortion to your sound by carefully aimed soft palette filtering. The following section will assist you develop a variety of vocal approaches for rock.

## Growling

By adding a simple, safe-throat noise to the beginning of each lyrical phrase, you can add a new dimension to your vocal style. This technique works well for rock ballads as well as fast rock. With a small amount of practice, you will be delivering unique rock sounds with this technique.

## Exercise Two

Start by singing a low, but comfortable, 'argh' sound. Ensure the tone is effortless and it does not have a breathy quality. Spend time going over the sound several times, gradually reducing the volume with each attempt. When your sound is at its absolute minimum volume, without being breathy, create a growl sound (like a dog). You will notice a slight 'rumble' toward the back of your throat. Practise this several times to familiarise yourself with this new sound. As you practise there should be no tension, discomfort or dryness of the throat. The growl should not be forced. Don't worry if you cannot achieve this sound straight away as it may take a little practice.

Now take a line from a song of your choice (a lower pitched line is easiest to begin with). At the beginning of the very first syllable, recreate the growl and allow this sound to lead into the first note. The growl sound will last a fraction of a second, but will add a unique style to the delivery of the note. Try adding the growl to each word in the line. Depending on both the style of the music and your personal taste, you can use this delivery style as much or as little as is required within a song.

**KEY POINTS**

* sing a low 'argh' sound

* gradually reduce the volume with each attempt

* notice the subtle growl that occurs in the throat at lowest volumes

* add this growl sound to the beginning of a word from a song

* ensure there is no tension, discomfort or dryness of the throat as you practise

* experiment with various styles of rock using this technique

## *Horizontal Positioning*

As discovered in previous chapters, the shape of the mouth dramatically affects the produced sound. A vertical open shape gives a more traditional pure sound, whilst a horizontal wide smile shape will produce a more 'twangy' sound that can be taken to the extremes in a rock performance. The following exercise will highlight two approaches to utilising this harsher sound in your performances. Whilst practising, you should maintain a low volume to feel the effects of facial filtering without allowing too much volume and pressure to obscure the results.

## Exercise Three

Using a few lines from your chosen song, practise singing with a wide smile and keep your teeth tightly together. You will feel a slight vibration in the top of your cheeks and may notice that some of the sound becomes slightly nasal sounding. After practising like this for at least ten minutes, create the same sensations as you deliver the lines without your teeth together. Notice how the sound stays harsh but does not create any discomfort in the throat. You are using your face as a distortion tool for the safe sound that the larynx has created.

Now replace each syllable of the words with the sound 'ung'. Again, practise this for at least ten minutes and notice how the nasal cavity has now been implemented to a greater extent. It has created a different variety of distortion for your sound. Sing the words again, creating the same sensations in your face to filter the sound in the same way as with 'ung'.

### KEY POINTS

* horizontal shaping gives a harsher tone

* practise your song with a wide smile a teeth tightly together

* create the same sensation as you sing without teeth together

* sing the lines of the song replacing each syllable with 'ung'

* notice the increased nasal quality of the tone

* create the same sensations as you sing the words

## *The Rock Scream*

Welcome to the danger zone: proceed at your own risk! The rock scream will go down in history as the biggest cause of voice damage ever. Be aware of this as you practise the technique and ensure that practice is stopped immediately if any discomfort, fatigue or tickling sensations occur. The following exercise will take you through a low impact technique to maximise the sound and minimise stress on the larynx. The object of the technique is to create a single sound that can be used as a scream-type effect between lyrics. It is not designed for use on general lyrics or for any prolonged period during a song.

# Exercise Four

Start by singing a high, but comfortable and quiet, 'wah' sound. This sound can be done with the 'real voice' or 'falsetto' (refer to previous chapters if you require clarification of these terms). The start of the sound should emanate from a tight pursed lip position (as if you are about to whistle) and then moved into a wide hori-zontal shape. Repeat the sound in rapid succession to get used to the feeling of this muscle movement. Once you are happy with this sensation, begin to increase the volume. You should feel that the mouth is doing most of the work and the throat stays reason-ably relaxed. If you prefer a more definite ending to your sound change from 'wah' to 'wow' at this point. Gradually and slowly, build up the volume ensuring that the scream stays controlled and comfortable (unlike a typical natural scream).

### KEY POINTS

* ✶ pay close attention to your vocal stress and keep safe

* ✶ sing a 'wah' sound using the correct shaping

* ✶ repeat the sound in rapid succession to get used to the sensation

* ✶ gradually and safely, increase the volume

* ✶ feel that the mouth is doing the work, not the throat!

## *Resonate Depth*

Resonate Depth involves quickly changing between resonating cavities on a single note. The effect of this change creates an interesting blend of tones for the audience. It will add character and excitement to your performance.

This process is very similar to the GROWLING technique but involves a fast change of resonance, rather than adding new sounds. If you are fully familiar with Chest, Head and Mouth/Nasal resonance from previous chapters, then this exercise will utilise your skills to create further interesting and unique sounds.

# Exercise Five

Sing a comfortable chest tone to the sound of 'argh'. You will now evolve this sound (at the same pitch) into other resonate areas. If you wish to make the sound resonate toward the head, change the sound to 'dor'. If you wish to make the sound resonate toward the mouth, change the sound to 'ay'.

Hold a single sound and allow the resonate changes to transition smoothly without any breaks or lumps in the tone. Experiment slowly with combinations of resonance and gradually make the changes happen closer together. When you apply this approach to the lyrics, it may be useful to utilise the natural sound of the word to help decide where to resonate (i.e. the word 'away' could be chest into mouth.) Start by singing the line of the song slowly, working on individual words and then build up speed until you can deliver the line at full speed with a variety of dramatic resonance.

**KEY POINTS**

* ensure you are familiar with resonating cavities from previous chapters

* slowly sing a tone altering the way it is resonating as you sing

* speed up your resonate changes

* apply resonate changes to each individual word in your song

* experiment with various styles of rock using this technique

## Dynamic stability

We associate high levels of power with rock music. Before performing a song, it is important to look at the dynamic structure so that you can deliver it in the best possible way to suit your vocal style. Consider where the sections of high volume or aggression occur and decide whether the remaining sections of the song contrast enough to make these louder sections appear to have more impact. It may be beneficial to reduce the volume of a verse just to make the chorus seem even louder. This relative change in volume will give the illusion of a more powerful and interesting performance. Audiences respond to dynamic changes in a song, so if you sing the whole thing at full volume it will become monotonous and the audience will not consider you a powerful performer.

## Myths

In your quest to find out what gives your favourite performer their unique sound, you will inevitably be subjected to some of the most bizarre and dangerous pieces of advice. Do not believe everything you hear, even if it comes from a great performer. Rock musicians can be a theatrical bunch of people. They often say things for shock value. Over the years I have heard some of the silliest ways to create a rock sound which are all based on myth and have no true value or substance whatsoever...apart from, perhaps, to raise a smile. Despite the obvious stupidity of the suggestions, some vocalists still try them. This can cause vocal damage as well as making oneself look completely foolish. Here are some of the crazy techniques that I have heard about – these are for your amusement only and definitely should not be tried – EVER! "I drink a bottle of brandy before every performance to give my voice an edge"

"I mix a raw egg with a pint of water and add a shot of vodka. This lubricates my throat"

"I chain smoke a whole pack of cigarettes before the show so I sound rougher"

"I scream until it hurts and then my voice sounds gruffer"

This is my absolute favourite from a rock singer I interviewed for a TV show…

"I eat several meat pies before I sing and the pastry rattles in my throat giving me a unique sound"

## In The Studio

Finally, I would like to make you aware of some of the studio (and live) effects that are used by rock vocalists. These tools can create strange and wonderful sounds that can add to an overall performance. If you just cannot seem to create the sound of your favourite artist, it may be because they get a little helping hand from technology.

**GATE EFFECT:** This tool can cut the beginning and end of each sound to give a high level of vocal attack.

**CHORUS:** A favourite with rock vocalists as it can make the voice sound thicker, harsher or even make it sound like there is more than one vocalist.

**DOUBLE TRACKING**: This is when a singer records the vocal twice, or more, and the recordings are played back together to strengthen and thicken the sound.

**DISTORTION:** This effect has been used by guitarists for a long time and can be applied to the voice to get a rougher sound.

**DELAY:** This can have a similar effect to CHORUS or DOUBLE TRACKING if slight delay is used.

**REVERB**: A type of subtle echo that can simulate the singer being in a particular environment. This effect is often used on all genres of vocal recording.

**PITCH-CORRECTION:** This effect was designed to fix out-of-tune vocals, but is now often used to expand a singer's range electrically.

See the more extensive studio terminology list in the chapter 'Recording A Demo'.

# Chapter completion checklist

Keep returning to the exercises in this chapter throughout your vocal development. You have successfully completed this chapter if you can agree with all of the statements below.

✓ I understand the potential vocal health issues related to 'Rock' style singing

✓ I understand and can demonstrate vocal attack

✓ I understand where to direct sound in order to use soft palette filtering

✓ I can alter my vocal sound with the 'growl'

✓ I can create 'rock' sounds with horizontal mouth shapes

✓ I understand the dangers of the 'rock scream'

✓ I am able to change resonance on a single note

✓ I understand how power is demonstrated by dynamic performance

# YOUR NOTES

# Chapter Fourteen

# Speed Singing, Rap and MC

Whether you want to develop a strong rap technique, or perform fast, freestyle musical passages like Christina and Mariah, it is important to have a clear rhythmical understanding and flow. During this chapter you will be developing your rhythm skills, improving the clarity of your words at speed and creating a personal daily practice schedule to help you achieve fast results.

Owing to the vast array of speed singing styles, including Rap, MC, Scat, Freestyle and R&B, it is in the best interest of any vocalist to familiarise themselves with the art and practice of speed singing. Due to the nature of this type of performance, all lyrics should be learned and memorised to ensure that your reading speed does not affect the performance.

## *The Art of Rhythm*

At this point you may wish to recap on the techniques and explanation of rhythm from the 'Get With The Beat' chapter. Rather than practising an entire song, it is far better to work on your speed singing with short phrases. The basic approach to fitting words, at speed, into the music, will be to work with four types of short rhythmical phrases.

The first, and easiest, is a single note. We will represent this note by using the word 'rap'. If you clap this word, there is only one clap. The second involves a pair of notes in quick succession that we will represent by the word 'doctor' (two claps). The third is a triplet, which is three notes in quick succession represented by the word 'elephant' (three claps).

The fourth is four notes in quick succession represented by the word 'incredible' (four claps).

## Exercise One

Find a song or piece of music with a clear beat (ideally without any vocals). As you listen to the music, try to fit each of the rhythmical words into the beat of the music. Start slowly, and gradually mix and match the words at speed. Experiment with a variety of music and try substituting the suggested words with ideas of your own. Can you think of a five-syllable word to take the exercise on a step further? This exercise can be practised along with most music and should be included in your daily practice. You can practise along with songs on the radio or your favourite CD.

**KEY POINTS**

* familiarise yourself with the rhythmical words

* find a piece of music with a clear beat

* fit the rhythmical words over the beat of the music

* speed up your delivery of the words

* experiment with other backing music and other rhythmical words

During the previous exercise, you will have noticed that the pitch of the words was not taken into consideration. Like a percussive instrument, you just created beats with the rhythmical words. The following exercise works in a similar way but uses every day speech fitted into the beat of the music. Rap is essentially a story or point of view spoken at speed over music. Rap often rhymes but this is not necessary, it is more about creating a flow of words in a rhythm that fits the music.

## Exercise Two

Using a paragraph of text (perhaps from this book), read the words over the top of a musical beat. Start slowly and try to fit each syllable of your text in with the beat of the music.

It may help to start each sentence on the first count of each four-count pattern (assuming your music is using a standard four-count pattern). Once you are comfortable with this, try doubling or halving the speed of your speech, making sure that the words still fit in with the flow of the music. This exercise improves your general rhythmical awareness and allows you the freedom to experiment with rhythmical variation.

**KEY POINTS**

* decide on a paragraph of text to read

* find a piece of music with a clear beat

* speak your paragraph over the beat of the music

* experiment with timing - halve and double the speed of delivery

During the previous two exercises, you may have found yourself tripping over words and/or not delivering the words with enough clarity. This is will improve with continued practice. Do not be afraid to make mistakes. The following section will help you focus on faster and more accurate mouth and tongue movement. This will speed up the process of developing clarity and impact.

## *Let's Twist*

Tongue twisters are the obvious choice for getting your mouth moving faster and more accurately. These childlike passages are often underestimated. With regular practice, tongue twisters can lead to a high level of clarity in both speech and song. Below are some examples for you to practise. You may find additional tongue twisters on various internet sites. Start practising each tongue twister slowly and repeat it over and over again, whilst gradually increasing the delivery speed.

*Example 1. Rubber, Baby, Buggy, Bumpers*

*Example 2. The tip of the tongue, the teeth and the lips*

*Example 3. Lesser leather never weathered better weather better*

*Example 4. Mrs Smith's Fish Sauce Shop*

In addition to tongue twisters, another technique dramatically improves the mobility of the tongue for improved delivery of fast vocals. Place a pen or pencil horizontally in your mouth (each end should be outside of your mouth like a dog holding a bone). Hold it in place with your back teeth (Do not bite too hard!). With the pencil in place, read a passage of text. During this practice, your tongue will need to become more mobile in order for your speech to make any sense at all. Practise the pencil technique for ten minutes each day and you will soon notice that you have a far better clarity in all aspects of your vocal work.

## Shape Switches of the Pharynx

In basic terms, the pharynx is the back of the throat. It starts behind the nose and goes down to the larynx (voice box). During fast singing, we can emphasise pharynx movement and quickly shape sound. Think about artists like Whitney Houston and Mariah Carey. They perform fast vocals, adding a huge 'show off' factor to their performances. During this section, you will be learning to feel and understand pharynx movements. This will help you direct and control sound further.

# Exercise One

During this section, you will be singing a pitched sound that is in a comfortable and strong area of your vocal range. Start with an 'argh' sound and shape your mouth appropriately to achieve a pure sound (as in previous chapters). Here is where the big change in approach occurs. In previous chapters, I have been encouraging you to dramatically shape the front of your mouth in order to improve the sound quality. This time, in order to feel the pharynx movement, you will need to keep the mouth locked in the initial position throughout.

Whilst maintaining the same, comfortable pitch, change the 'argh' sound to an 'or' sound. Concentrate on the movement and 'shape shift' at the back of your throat as you do this. The work of the pharynx should now be obvious to you. Practise speeding up the change from 'argh' to 'or' and repeatedly change between these sounds as you sing a note.

- sing an initial 'argh' sound and maintain a good mouth shape

- change between 'argh' and 'or' as you hold the sound

- concentrate on the movement of the pharynx as you practise

- ensure the front of your mouth is not moving

- repeatedly change between sounds whilst holding a note

# Exercise Two

During this exercise you will be stepping up and down through pitches whilst experiencing the movement of the Pharynx. Pay close attention to the sensations that occur. Start by singing a comfortable 'argh' high sound. This sound should be easy and not at the top of your range where there may be a risk of tension occurring. Now slowly step down through the pitches until you reach the lower, comfortable area of your range. As you change between pitches, alternate between the 'argh' and 'or' sounds (remember to keep your mouth shape the same). As you become more competent, increase the speed of the exercise.

**KEY POINTS**

- sing an initial high 'argh' sound and maintain a good mouth shape

- change between 'argh' and 'or' as you step down slowly through pitches

- concentrate on the movement of the pharynx as you practise

- ensure the front of your mouth is not moving

- increase the speed of the exercise

Once you are familiar with the sensations of pharynx movement, sing an entire song whilst keeping your mouth in the same position. Notice how the back of your throat feels like it is changing position in a similar way to mouth shapes. Good pharynx control combined with mouth shaping will lead to greatly improved tones and a higher degree of vocal agility.

## Chapter completion checklist

Keep returning to the exercises in this chapter throughout your vocal development. You have successfully completed this chapter if you can agree with all of the statements below.

✓ I have understood the importance of rhythm and clarity for this genre

✓ I am well practiced at fitting various size note groupings into an established rhythm

✓ I practise speed technique with tongue twisters

✓ I am able to 'shape shift' my pharynx

# YOUR NOTES

YOUR NOTES

Chapter Fifteen

# Microphone Technique

A microphone (mic) is not only there to make you louder, it can be used to positively affect your overall performance. Professional singers must be aware that a microphone is an important tool of their craft. Microphone familiarisation and technique should become part of your daily practice. No matter how gifted you are at producing a good vocal, correct microphone technique will give you a major advantage in the process of developing the sound you want. This chapter will explain how to get the best from your sound with a microphone, and provide you with an explanation of microphone specification and microphone types.

## *Setting Up Your Sound*

When you purchase a microphone, ensure that you have a lead to connect it to your amplification equipment (mixer and amplifier). Often leads need to be purchased separately. Once connected, check the microphone is operating correctly by singing a line of a song. If you are happy that the microphone is operating well, switch the microphone off. Now play your backing track and set this to the desired volume level. When the backing track is set and playing, switch the microphone back on and set its volume so that you can be clearly heard over the top of the backing track. If you cannot determine the desired volume, gradually reduce the volume of the backing track until your voice is clear. You may decide that 'equalisation' or 'effects' are now needed on the microphone. Refer to your mixer/amp literature if you are unsure how to do this.

## *Holding Your Microphone*

There are many schools of thought on best practice when holding a microphone. The most important thing is to make friends with your microphone and become comfortable using it. Many people feel that microphones are intimidating and, as a result, do not like to get too close. This defeats the purpose of trying to get your voice clearly heard. Spend time getting used to the sound of your amplified voice.

Ensure that you have a firm grip on the body/shaft of the microphone. If you hold a microphone loosely, there is a chance that the noise from the 'body' moving in your hand will be picked up and amplified. Do not allow any part of your hand to touch the pickup area (usually the mesh part). This will affect the microphone's clarity, pickup and will increase the risk of feedback (see below).

Start by holding the microphone approximately three to four inches away from your mouth. This distance may need to be adjusted slightly to achieve the best sound. Most vocalists prefer to hold the microphone at a slight angle (as opposed to straight in front of the mouth). This ensures that 'air bursts' from certain syllables (typically b's and p's) do not hit the microphone directly. As mentioned in previous chapters, blasts of air can cause sudden unwanted pops and noise.

## Feedback

Feedback is a sound that can happen if a microphone is set too loud and/or is very close to the speaker. This occurs when the sound produced by the speakers is picked up in the microphone, which causes a 'loop' in the system resulting in an unwanted, loud piercing howl. Other factors that make feedback more likely to occur include how the microphone is held, the shape and size of the performance space, microphone type, and amplifier type. Both speaker and microphone positioning within a room will affect the likelihood of feedback. Experiment with different set-up positions if feedback occurs. To reduce the risk of feedback, it is essential that you 'sound-check' your system using the setup procedure before every performance.

## Volume Tricks

The distance from the microphone to the performer's mouth will have a direct impact on how loudly they are amplified. As a performer, this is a useful tool when needing to gain further control of dynamics. Practise fading in and out long notes using only microphone distance and balance the overall sound by keeping the microphone close for quiet sections, and further away for louder notes. By doing this you will be able to control the 'mix' of your voice with the music at all times, without the need to be close to the mixer and amp. Take time to experiment with microphone distancing to ensure that your tones are not lost (too far away from the microphone) or distorted (too close to the microphone).

## Equalisation Tricks –Proximity Effect

The proximity effect is a term used to describe how the equalisation (treble & bass) of sound changes with distance from the microphone. Experiment with how your voice changes in tone at various microphone distances. The closer you are to the microphone, the more bass will be apparent in your tone. Use this effect to further shape and enhance the sound of your voice across all resonating cavities.

## Using Distortion

Some 'rock' vocalists create a harsh distorted sound on purpose by holding the microphone close to, or against their mouth. Some even cover the sides of the mesh part with their hand. As mentioned earlier in this chapter, this is not best practice and has the potential to damage your equipment. If distortion is required, it would be wiser to purchase a 'distortion effect unit' from a studio equipment supplier. These suppliers can easily be found on the internet and will often provide information and advice.

## Adding Effects to Your Microphone

During performances, it is very unusual for a vocalist to have a dry (without effects) sound. Effects are sometimes built into mixing desks (check your operating instructions), or can be purchased as separate units to plug into existing equipment. The most common types of effect in live performance are reverbs, delays, gates, compression and chorus (refer to the 'recording a demo' chapter if you need to familiarise yourself with these terms). During my own live performances, I use a separate effects unit that provides a small amount of reverb only.

## Microphone Types

Vocalists should be aware of the two basic types of microphone: Condenser and Dynamic. The following information includes many 'technical' terms and a basic explanation of these terms is provided both here, and in the glossary. If you require a more detailed explanation, you will find many books dedicated to the vast, technical subject of electronics and audio acoustics.

**DYNAMIC MICROPHONES:** Dynamic microphones are most commonly used by singers for live performance. They can be used for studio recording situations too. A dynamic microphone is typically a lot more robust than other microphones. It is also simple to use. The performer needs to be close to a dynamic mic for optimal results. Dynamic mics do not require an external power supply or batteries when connected to a mixer. Inside a dynamic mic, there is a diaphragm attached to a coil of wire. This is suspended in a magnetic coil (just like a speaker). Sound hitting the diaphragm causes the coil to move which generates voltage. This voltage is sent down the cable to a mixer where it is amplified before being sent to the speaker. Because this physical coil movement requires lots of sound energy, dynamic mics are not always very clear at reproducing the subtle vibrations of high frequencies. For this reason, condenser mics are often preferred for studio recording.

**CONDENSER MICROPHONES:** Condenser microphones are highly sensitive and deliver good performances at a wider range of frequencies. They are used less in live situations as they are more fragile than dynamic mics (although improving technology is making this less of an issue). They operate on a small amount of voltage that is delivered through either a battery or 'Phantom Power'. Phantom Power is a separate power supply often built into mixers. If you are buying a condenser mic, check that you have the appropriate equipment to power it. Inside a condenser mic, two thin plates of metal are charged by the voltage. There is a space between the two plates. As sound hits the top plate, the resistance of the space changes and the resulting voltage is sent down the cable to a mixer where it is amplified before being sent to the speaker.

## *Understanding Microphone Specifications*

Below are some basic explanations of microphone specification. Please remember that although specifications give an indication of how well a microphone picks up sound, they will not give a total appreciation of how the microphone sounds in real situations.

### PICKUP PATTERNS
(Also known as 'Directionality' or 'Polar Response')

Most microphones will 'pick up' sound from a wide area. However, the sounds from outside the microphone's 'pickup pattern' will be detected at far lower levels. The pickup pattern diagram shown in microphone literature will give an indication of how well the microphone picks up sound frequency from different angles around the microphone.

* **'Uni-directional' or 'cardioid'** mics can pick up a wide spectrum of sound from the front but sound coming from the rear of the microphone is not picked up well. This makes this type of mic suitable for picking up a singer and not too much other surrounding noise.

* **'Hyper-cardioid'** and 'super-cardioid' mics are also in the uni-directional category. They pick up a narrower area in front of the mic, which cuts out even more unwanted background noise.

* **'Omni-directional'** mics pick up a wide range of frequencies from virtually 360 degrees around the mic. In other words, they pick up sounds well from all directions. These mics are less suitable for solo singers and are used for applications including: recording round-table meetings or audience ambience.

## *Frequency Response*

This is usually expressed as a diagram. It shows how well a microphone picks up different frequency sounds (highs and lows). Microphones do not pick up every frequency in exactly the same way due to the different vibrations of each frequency.

### Frequency Range

This gives a general indication of what range of sounds a microphone can pick up and is usually expressed in Hertz (Hz = a unit of sound frequency). As a guide, most humans can hear sounds in the range of 20Hz (very low pitch) to 20 kHz (very high pitch).

### Maximum Sound Pressure

Loudness is measured in decibels (dB). The maximum sound pressure indicates the maximum volume a microphone can handle.

## Chapter completion checklist

Keep returning to the exercises in this chapter throughout your vocal development. You have successfully completed this chapter if you can agree with all of the statements below.

✓ I understand that good microphone technique is vital as a professional performer

✓ I am able to set up my microphone and test the level of my vocal with the backing track

✓ I know how to hold a microphone correctly

✓ I understand why feedback occurs

✓ I understand how to adjust the volume of my vocal by distancing the microphone

✓ I know how condenser and dynamic microphones differ from each other

✓ I have a basic understanding of microphone manufacturers' specifications

# YOUR NOTES

# Chapter Sixteen

# Vocal Identity And Design

Most professional vocalists know that success, as a new, memorable performing artist, requires a unique sound. One of the most common things I hear vocal students talk about is developing such a sound. This chapter will help you understand how to find and reach your own capabilities so that you may have a wealth of tonal quality to shape and develop your own style.

If you have already decided that you are a vocalist of a particular genre, I would like you now to be ready to embrace all styles (even the obscure and old fashioned.) Awareness and appreciation of other genres will greatly assist you in developing your own style and versatility. Limiting your performance style at an early stage of your development will stop the growth and potential of your final sound.

## *Understanding Timbre Within A Genre*

A musical arranger's job is to find the best sounds to give a song the desired overall sound. Decisions like which type of instruments, how many instruments and combinations of sounds, all have to be made in order to achieve a good result. The tonal quality of an instrument gives a particular flavour to the song and helps to define its genre. Think of some genres of music and you will immediately think of instruments associated with that genre (e.g. dance music may have a strong bass, folk music may have acoustic guitar).

Depending on the musical arrangement, your vocal tone as a performer may need to adjust to blend with the musical arrangement. Your vocal timbre (tone of voice), will have a direct effect on the overall sound and must be considered carefully. Listen to a variety of music and decide how the voice fits with the arrangement (i.e. is the tone high frequency, is it full and round?) Musical notes and timing have an effect on genre, but the key to creating the desired overall sound is timbre.

## Experimenting With Timbre

During previous chapters we have discussed the importance of achieving a sound that is different to other performers. Although it may seem like a contradiction, to achieve this we must experiment with the sounds of others. To clarify this point, imagine this example:

You have been asked to write a romance novel and you have not done anything like this before. Your first step would be to read as many romance novels as possible to get an idea of story structure and both good and bad writing practice. You then use all of this 'research' to devise your own unique story and structure. You use flavours from a variety of other works and ensure you avoid elements that did not appeal to you. The result is a unique story and writing style, made from experience of, and exposure to, other works.

From the example above we can understand how new ideas come directly from experience and an understanding of what has come before. The best way to achieve this as a performing artist is by mimicking the sounds of others. Your aim should not be to get a perfect duplication of sound, but simply to understand the vocal placement of others to produce a sound close to the style of artist you are studying. Do not be tempted to study artists only from the genre that interests you. This will not create the total awareness you require. Make efforts to experiment with genres that are far removed from your chosen style as these are the most likely to stretch and surprise you.

## Identifying Vocal Qualities

Below are some key factors in recreating sounds of others. Check each of the following as you work on your sounds:

**Range** – What is the highest and lowest note of the artist you are mimicking? Will you need to work on exercises in this book in order to reach the desired notes? Are any notes falsetto?

**Timing** – Does the artist have tight or loose timing? In other words, does each note fall on an obvious beat or is the timing very loose and relaxed? Which words in the phrase have emphasis?

*Accent* – Does the artist have an obvious accent? Are any of the words pronounced differently to your natural performance style? Are vowel sounds changed for any words to assist delivery of the material?

*Placement* – Using your experience and practice of resonating cavities, work out how the artist places each sound. Do they use the same resonation throughout or is it altered across sections or even individual notes?

*Attack* – How are the notes started? Are they hit hard like a percussive sound, joined to other notes smoothly, or are there volume or pitch slides into notes?

*Sustain* – How long are notes held for and how are they held? Does the artist use vibrato or keep the sound smooth? Are notes staccato or legato?

*Decay* – How do notes end? Do they cut off or fade out?

*Effects* – Are there any effects used on the voice? Is the vocal sound electronically processed in any way? Is it possible to emulate this effectively in a natural way? Are you sure you are listening to only one voice or has the vocal been 'doubled' for effect?

Vocal Hooks – A hook is any interesting or memorable reoccurring detail in the vocal style, almost like a trademark e.g. Mariah Carey and her detailed, frequent ad-libs.

## *Using Your New Experience*
After experimenting and mastering a variety of vocal textures, you will be able to sing your songs utilising your new experience. This will give more dynamic emphasis and identity to the song. During the process of learning other styles, you will have also worked and developed your voice in new exciting ways, strengthening your natural tone.

Vocal confidence and versatility also increase greatly after devoting time to this experimentation. Make experimentation a part of your ongoing practice.

## Designing Your Voice

After developing all the resonating cavities, singers usually ask 'how do I know when to use each resonating area or particular technique'. It is important to point out that there are no definitive right or wrong answers to this. Producing a great vocal tone is about creativity and comfort. The more you practise a technique, the more likely you are to feel comfortable enough to add it to your performance. For example - when learning to drive, there are thousands of decisions to make. Any new driver considers the whole process to be a little overwhelming, but after practice, controlling a vehicle becomes almost second nature. The same applies to singing.

If you have to think hard about how to achieve the best sound, then you are a very good student, but not quite ready to be launching into a professional career. Allow yourself the time to practise in order to become a more natural singer. Ensure you are thoroughly prepared before moving on to the remainder of this chapter. You have more chance of success when you are fully ready!

# Exercise One

By now, you will have some idea of what style of music you would like to be performing. You will not want to limit yourself with this style, but as a starting point, find a song that you know and sing well. It will be necessary to record each stage of this exercise.

Do not rush the exercise. It will take several days to complete successfully. Record the verse of your chosen song several times. Each attempt should involve adjusting the placement of the sound by altering the resonating cavity. Repeat the process again, this time add/remove some vocal effects like breathiness or hard attack. During the recording process, make written notes of what placement/effect you are employing. Once you have many variations on the recording then stop. Do not play back the recordings straight away.

During the various stages of recording, you will have made immediate decisions from your own perspective of what works and what does not. These decisions can often be wrong! Wait at least twenty-four hours before listening to the recording. Do not look at your notes prior to listening.

Let your ears decide what sounds good first and then check your notes to find out how you achieved those sounds.

Repeat this entire exercise as often as possible with various songs.

**KEY POINTS**

* decide on material that you are comfortable singing

* record various approaches to a small section of the song and make notes on how you create each sound

* wait at least twenty-four hours before listening back to your work

* make decisions on what sounds best

* check your notes to see how you achieved the sound you prefer

# Chapter completion checklist

Keep returning to the exercises in this chapter throughout your vocal development. You have successfully completed this chapter if you can agree with all of the statements below.

✓ I understand that developing a unique sound is an important part of becoming a professional vocalist

✓ I am aware of the need to attempt new styles of singing

✓ I understand the importance of vocal timbre within a song

✓ I am aware that developing my experience of other vocal styles will improve my ability to create a unique sound

✓ I understand how to examine other vocalists' techniques

✓ I have experimented with many different genres and artists

# YOUR NOTES

# YOUR NOTES

Chapter Seventeen

# Auditions

As a performer, auditions are inevitable. They occur across all fields of performing arts. On rare occasion, reputation or past performances may be all that is required to secure a record deal or a part in the latest musical theatre hit show. However, throughout your career as a vocalist, you should always be prepared and happy to audition. Even highly paid, successful 'known' artists still need to audition from time to time.

An audition is an opportunity for you to show that you are capable, and for the audition panel to consider whether you can be part of their planned future venture. An audition panel will generally have a firm idea of their vision. Success and failure is not as straightforward as who sings the best. Many other elements are considered when choosing artists.

This chapter will help prepare you to have the best possible opportunity when putting yourself forward for audition. It will cover general advice for all auditions.

## Types of Audition
There are three main types of audition: open, private (closed), call-back.

An open audition is often advertised in the media or specialist artist forums. This type of audition is open to everyone and usually attracts many people. When attending an open audition, be prepared to wait around for a very long time as the panel will take time to see everyone.

A private or closed audition will give you a specific time for an audition that is different to other people. These auditions are for invited artists only and generally involve less waiting around. It is always a good idea to allow plenty of time for any audition even if it is private.

Call-back auditions are subsequent auditions. These are the result of the panel taking an interest in you after a first audition. The panel will have discarded other artists and will only be inviting those back who impressed initially.

## Which audition?

Auditions require practice in order for you to feel completely relaxed and show your full potential. With this in mind try to attend as many auditions as possible. Remember that if you are selected, it is still your choice to accept or decline a position. Many artists audition for work that does not really excite them in order to gain as much audition experience as possible.

## When to Audition

If you are able to choose a time for your audition, try to get an early slot. Audition panels get tired and will generally be more positive at the start of their shift.

## Research

Whatever you are auditioning for, ensure that you do as much research as possible. Thoroughly read any audition material details you have. If you are auditioning for a musical theatre show, find out what the show is and look at other material within the show that you think you could also be considered for. Even if you are auditioning for a specific role, audition panels are usually casting for other roles too and may suggest you could play another part. If possible, find out who the panel are. Any panel member will be pleased if you are familiar their work. They are artists too and recognition feeds their ego well. Finding out what type of artists they have selected for other shows may also help you in choosing your approach.

## Audition Attitude

An audition starts from the moment you walk into the building. Panels will look at the personality and demeanour of potential acts as well as their ability to interact with others. Bitchy or unfriendly behaviour towards others auditioning, will prove that you are not suitable to work in a show team and can end your chances at the audition. Always be friendly and courteous.

It is important to ensure that you are on time and prepared for any audition. Allow extra time for your journey so that you will still be on time if traffic is bad or trains are delayed. If you are going to be late, make a phone call to see if your audition is still possible and to keep the panel informed.

Never make excuses at auditions. If you are under prepared, take responsibility and do not blame others. An audition panel does not want to know what you could do if you were more prepared or in better health, they want to see and hear what you can do now. If you are unwell, a panel will hear this in your performance and make a judgement accordingly. It is not professional to make excuses at any time, for any reason, during auditions.

If rejected there and then, continue to be polite and courteous. Thank the panel for their time and leave gracefully. Arguing or insisting on reasons for rejection will make you look unprofessional and silly. Panel members may also be at other auditions and will remember a bad attitude.

## Choosing Your Audition Material

Read any brief that you have been given before an audition to ensure that you choose suitable material. Choose material that shows off your power, range and identity. If your audition is for a musical theatre show, you will often be asked to prepare two contrasting songs. One song should be a ballad, the other more up-tempo. Try to find songs that contrast in emotion as well as speed. However many songs you prepare, ensure (where possible) that you start with your strongest. If you choose a musical theatre song, make sure that you are familiar with the show that the song is from.

Do not be disheartened if you are stopped a short way into your song. With a large number of people to audition, it is common practice to hear only a small section of a song. This does not mean that you have failed or have sung badly. Sometimes an audition panel will ask you to prepare two or more songs but will only hear a section of one song; this is also common practice and not something to cause concern.

Find out what backing options are available to you at the audition. Some auditions will allow you to take a CD backing track. Some will provide a pianist and you will need to take sheet music. Many open auditions for vocalists are now completely acapella and you will sing unaccompanied. If sheet music is required, make sure that it is in the right key and that the copy is neatly presented.

DO NOT TAKE PHOTOCOPIED SHEET MUSIC. There are many online sheet music suppliers. Most of these suppliers allow you to preview and change the key of the music. They will also grant you the proper licence to print the sheet music at home. This is by far the most cost effective way of purchasing individual songs in sheet music format. Take your contact information to leave with the panel or any other potential contact.

## *Choose Your Approach*
To eliminate unnecessary stress, ensure that audition songs are fully rehearsed.

Plan your delivery of the song in terms of dynamics, placement, character and emotion. Plan every detail so that you have points to focus on if you become nervous.

Before your audition, remind yourself of what is required for a good representation of your sound. Be loud and clear. Nervousness can often cause a reduction in volume and a 'shy' delivery. Ensure your first note is of your usual standard and the rest should follow. Look focused and confident by keeping your hands still and your eyes focused.

Nervousness can often cause us to look slightly down. Be aware of this and keep your eyes level or slightly looking upward. If you make a mistake during your delivery, pick the song up again as soon as you can and continue with confidence. Do not make an 'I made a mistake' expression and do not apologise during the song.

When entering an audition room, it is important to look confident. Keep your head up and walk with purpose. Present the panel with a smile and a confident greeting. You may be asked some general questions before singing. These will usually be friendly 'ice-breaker' questions (e.g. 'where did you travel from?' or 'how long have you been singing?').

## *Positive Rejection & Continuation*

Audition panels will often say that making a final decision is tough. This is very true. Do not be too disheartened if you are not successful. Decisions will be made for a variety of reasons. A panel may have one hundred singers who can sing perfectly. This is when decisions on look, character, and availability come into play. Most of the time, rejections are simply the result of not quite fitting a specific profile rather than being bad. Like many very successful artists, you may experience lots of rejection before you hit the big time!

# Chapter completion checklist

Keep returning to the exercises in this chapter throughout your vocal development. You have successfully completed this chapter if you can agree with all of the statements below.

✓ I understand the three types of audition

✓ I understand that I should accrue audition experience

✓ I understand the importance of research before an audition

✓ I understand the importance of carefully selecting audition songs

✓ I know how to prepare for audition

✓ I realise the importance of my demeanour throughout the audition experience

## Chapter Eighteen

# Performance

A great vocalist is not always a great performer. Performance is a separate issue and needs to be carefully considered. Several factors may become obstacles for a good performance. This chapter is dedicated to identifying and removing such obstacles. Performance is all about one important factor - the audience. Without an audience, there cannot be a performance. As such, without a good performance, there is limited or no option for progression as a vocal artist. Later in the chapter, we will be discussing options for dealing with confidence issues, stage nerves, and taking command. First, let us look at audience awareness and expectation.

## *Understanding Your Audience*

As a performing artist in 'live' situations, you will quickly realise that no two audiences are the same. What works well one day may work less well on another day, even though the performances are almost identical. This can be very difficult to understand and sometimes disheartening. The following sections explain some possible causing factors. Your understanding of each will help you to manage each performance.

*Demographic* – The age and type of person making up your audience is an important factor in focusing your act. For example, a top quality rock band may never find success with an audience of elderly jazz fans. Look at your performance style and work out which types of people are your target audience. Try to find ways to adapt your act in the event that you find yourself in front of a different type of audience. Do some research and go to see a wide variety of music acts perform. At each performance, look at the demographic of the audience and see how various types of audience react.

*Expectation/Occasion* – Before attending a performance, audience members decide what type of event they are expecting. Ideally, the performer will aim to exceed expectation. Managing expectations can be tricky. If an audience is informed of what type of performance is happening, they will be in a far better state of mind to appreciate the performer. Ensure advertising is accurate and gives a good representation of the act. Keep advertising information brief so that the audience is more open to anything that might occur. If you are playing at a special occasion (i.e. a wedding or birthday party) then the audience will generally be open to any type of performance that allows them to express their happiness. It may be wise to reduce or remove any serious slow ballads (unless this type of music is specifically requested).

*Audience Size* – People act very differently in crowds. This makes audience size a factor to consider. If a gig attracts only a handful of people, they will usually be more open to sitting and listening to all types of music. If there are many people within close proximity of each other, they will generally want more excitement and up-tempo entertainment. One hundred people in a small pub could create a great bustling atmosphere, whilst one hundred people in a large theatre or hall would create much less of an atmosphere for enjoyment. This may even seem like a disappointing turnout, putting people off from attending future performances. Always plan your venues well. Start small, as it is far better for your reputation if you appear popular and fill venues.

*Comparable Talent* – If performing alongside other acts, an audience will judge you in direct comparison to others performing in the same show. Always ensure that your act provides something memorable and different.

## Relationship With An Audience

As a performing artist, you must develop a relationship with your audience within seconds. An audience will expect you to be in command. They trust you to guide the entertainment and deliver an emotional experience. A nervous or unsure performance leaves an audience insecure, uncomfortable and less able to enjoy the show.

Always remember that as a performer, you are in full control of the audience. Think of yourself as a host. Enter and exit the performance space with confidence and purpose. Speak clearly and make every word and gesture strong. Even if your performance is lacking in musicality, an audience will maintain their trust in you if your confidence remains strong.

## Managing Nerves

Nervous feelings before and during a performance affect every performer at some point in their career. These feelings prove that you care about your art. Sometimes the symptoms of nerves can affect a performance in a negative way. This is when we need to take steps to minimise the disruption. Remember, nervous symptoms can affect the whole body, but are initially generated by only one thing - the mind! Nervous feelings are quite simply an emotion. We can train ourselves to manage these emotions. Humans are great at adapting and refocusing emotion.

As an example, imagine you have just been told by a stranger that you are attractive. It has made you feel extremely good. Another stranger then tells you the same thing. If this continues to happen, you still feel pleased and appreciative, but you will be a lot less moved and happy than the first time. This is because you have learned to expect the experience. In the same way, we can learn what to expect of performance nerves and adapt to cope better. We are often shocked by how our body reacts to nerves, although the symptoms are generally the same each time. Make a list of all the things you think and feel when affected by nervousness. Look at each item on the list and give yourself permission to experience those symptoms. It is ok, and quite normal, to shake and feel slightly nauseous in these situations. If you know what symptoms to expect, you can deal with them better and not heighten the sensations by being shocked.

Nerves are also far less of a problem if proper preparation occurs. If you have practised your material enough, the risk of 'going wrong' is reduced and so is the apprehension associated with that possibility. Ensure that you are thoroughly prepared for any public performance and, where possible, rehearse in the final performance area. If this is not possible then rehearse in many different spaces so that you are comfortable with unfamiliar surroundings.

## *Practise Confidence*

Confidence needs to be practised. Often people with little confidence prefer to stick with a regular daily routine. Initial performances will be well outside this regular routine. The following exercise will help you gently challenge your own mind and boundaries.

# Exercise One

The best way to programme your own mind to deal comfortably with new situations is to present it with as many new situations as possible. As previously mentioned, this makes us grow accustomed to change and new challenges. At first, this exercise may seem childish and silly, but it has a profound effect on your subconscious mind. Every day for at least one week, do something strange that you have never done before. This experience will be private, and it is important that you feel free to do this without anyone else able to observe. The tasks you choose are products of your own imagination, they could range from trying a new activity to something as bizarre as wearing strange clothing for half an hour. The experience is simply about breaking out of your usual routine and does not need to have any other purpose, or make any sense to the rest of the world. Experiment with all sorts of things and make yourself smile with each task you set.

**KEY POINTS**

* do 'out-of-the-ordinary' tasks every day for at least one week

* do not try to be logical in your choice of tasks

The more you perform, the easier it will be to control your performance nerves. If you receive good feedback after a performance, you will gain control faster due to an increased self-belief.

## *'What's the worst that could happen?'*

Ask yourself the above question over and over again. If you sing badly, pass out or even throw up, you will feel bad for a few days but the rest of the world will carry on and not give it too much thought.

Let any mistakes drive you toward a better performance next time. After all, an artist is only as good as their last performance!

The stress of a performance can make it seem like it is the most important thing ever, but the truth is, there are other gigs and plenty of opportunities to shine. Yesterday's gig will be forgotten very quickly unless it is worth talking about for positive reasons!

# Chapter completion checklist

Keep returning to the exercises in this chapter throughout your vocal development. You have successfully completed this chapter if you can agree with all of the statements below.

✓ I understand the importance of my audience

✓ I understand and can explain factors that affect audiences

✓ I understand that I must take control in a performance

✓ I understand that confidence is an emotion

✓ I understand how to manage my performance nerves

# Chapter Nineteen

# The Fame Factor

What is that magical ingredient that pop stars have? Record companies and talent scouts always claim to be looking for that 'something special'. This chapter looks closely at a combination of factors that give a performer a competitive edge, and it goes way beyond having a 'nice' voice.

With a full understanding of yourself and how you can best present your talent, you will be in a much stronger position to impress everyone. Whether for an audition, a TV reality show, or demos for record companies, the understanding gained from this chapter will get you thinking creatively about the entire package that you can offer.

It is important to say at this stage that you are a product that you hope your audience will buy into. Your presence on stage and in your recordings evokes emotions within your audience. They will hopefully choose to relive those emotions by seeing or hearing your performance over and over again. Striking the right level of emotion at the right time is crucial to commercial success. Consider the five following elements (Acronym - TAG-IT) in relation to your own performance:

## TONE, APPEARANCE, GENRE, IDENTITY, TIMING

## *Element 1 – TONE*
Whilst studying the techniques in this book and experimenting with singing various styles of music, you will have noticed that your voice has a unique tonal quality. Because the voice is a unique instrument, your voice will have its own identity. There may be similarities to other performers but overall you should be creating a new sound. It is acceptable to roughly match your voice to a particular style of music, but do not assume that this limits your ability to perform other styles of music. Consider the quality of your tone in terms of purity, roughness, breathiness, or any unusual vocal traits. With careful experimentation, find out

if your vocal tone changes in style when singing vocals at different pitches. Do not be afraid to add slightly unnatural qualities to your voice in order to get a fresh sound (e.g. techniques learned in the 'Rock Tricks' chapter). Make a note of how you feel your voice sounds and ask friends to give their opinion of your vocal style. You will use these notes as reference when you sum up all your TAG-IT attributes at the end of this chapter.

## Element 2 – APPEARANCE

It is my strong belief that appearance is a crucial factor for any performing artist. This does not mean that you have to be 'drop-dead gorgeous', but you do need a look that is memorable and works with the music. Make a note of what you believe your clothes and general appearance say about you. Get honest opinions from others and find out what messages about your personality you are sending out by your appearance alone. Some artists, in the past, have highlighted some of their worst features in order to be remembered. Think about Aerosmith and that mouth, or Manilow's nose! Magazine beauty is all around, so how unique would you be if you looked like a stereotypical model? Do not focus on what you don't have - that just wastes time - focus on what you do have and what it says about you. Use the notes you have made for the TAG-IT summing up.

## Element 3 – GENRE

Music falls into many categories. Think of a selection of recording artists and you will be able to give a fairly general description of music that they produce (e.g. rock, soul, pop, classical). These different styles are referred to as genre. Whilst progressing through this book, you may already have decided what genre of music your voice is suited to. When approaching the subject of genre, an artist may find that their natural tonal quality fits well with music that may be different to their own personal taste. If this is the case, follow the exercises in this book to develop vocal characteristics that best suit your preferred genre. Just because you sound a particular way now, does not mean that you are stuck with it! Once you have decided on your ability to fall into a specific genre of music, then experiment with this style and try to push the boundaries of that style. 'Copycat' performances can be very entertaining, but you will need to bring something new in order to stand out from the crowd. Make notes about genres that you feel suit your vocal style and keep these for the TAG-IT summing up.

## Element 4 – IDENTITY

Whilst music itself creates some form of identity, it is also important for an artist to develop identity for commercial success. With the rise in popularity of reality TV shows, it is apparent that public opinion and votes for such shows go way beyond the talent displayed. The character, both on and off stage, of the performer is crucial to success. Think of these performers: Britney Spears, Michael Jackson, Lady Gaga, and Luciano Pavarotti. Without personally getting to know these people, we already have preconceived ideas about their personality. This helps them to give identity to the music they choose to perform. So what is your identity? How can you use your personal characteristics to strengthen your ability to perform? Like appearance, there are no set rules for identity. What may be considered to be a flaw in personality could end up being the key factor in creating success. Create a list of key words to sum up your identity and get friends and family to help too. Decide which areas can be highlighted further. Keep your list ready for the TAG-IT summing up.

## Element 5 – TIMING

Every genre of music has a mass of people who appreciate it. We could describe most genres as 'Popular Music' (Popular by definition means liked or appreciated by a mass of people). Music over time fits in with the trends of popular culture and often reflects the mood of the public.

For example, during World War II Vera Lynn was a hugely popular performance artist. Her song '(There'll Be Bluebirds Over) The White Cliffs of Dover' reflected the mood of the nation with its rousing lyrics that suggested hope for peace and highlighted the iconic cliffs as a symbol of pride for Britain. The timing of the release of this music undoubtedly played a huge role in its popularity. In the seventies, British people were generally feeling despondent about the state of British politics and the band 'The Sex

Pistols' were launched with their non-conformist approach and lyrical encouragement to create anarchy.

These examples show how looking at popular culture as a whole determines the success rate of music. Most music has a limited period of success. Deciding the right music at the right time is crucial to success. A common mistake made by new artists is to follow the musical trend and not take into account other areas of popular culture in order to strike with something fresh! Whilst it is impossible to be certain about future trends, it is well worth looking at successful artists and considering what it is about popular culture that has made them successful at that time. Draw up a list of possible cultural trends that are currently reflected in music; this may be useful in your TAG-IT summing up.

## Tag-It Summing Up

Now is the time to pull all of your lists and research together. Start by analysing other artists and seeing how their TAG-IT formula works and then start to develop your own TAG-IT profile. You may need to make adjustments to some of the elements in order to balance the overall result (e.g. an eccentric personality combined with love ballads and rock clothing would seem a little awkward and uncomfortable for most, but who knows? Maybe that's what the world has been waiting for!). Ensure that you feel comfortable that your overall performance package works for an audience and is marketable. Good Luck!

# Chapter completion checklist

Keep returning to the exercises in this chapter throughout your vocal development. You have successfully completed this chapter if you can agree with all of the statements below.

✓  I have understood and can explain TAG-IT

✓  I have researched how TAG-It applies to other successful artists

✓  I can relate TAG-IT to my own performance and vision

# YOUR NOTES

# YOUR NOTES

## Chapter Twenty

# Getting Started In The Music Business

This chapter is dedicated to helping you understand some of the many paths to gaining a career in music. If you have practised and completed all the chapters so far, you are obviously committed and prepared to take the challenging path to success. Bear in mind, there are no guarantees, however great your talent or how determined you are.

Before examining potential methods of generating success, I feel it is my duty to point out one of the biggest 'scams' for new recording artists. There are many companies who claim to be record labels, producers, talent scouts and so on. They may also claim to be affiliated with some well-known organisations. These companies offer auditions in great locations and will promise to make you a star! –BEWARE – Many of these companies will ask you to cover the costs of studio time or other production costs. No individual or company can ever guarantee you success and if such an organisation really wants to promote you, there will be no cost to you other than time! The above scam may also be run by genuine studios and is no more than a dishonest way of selling their studio time or song writing services. Always be very cautious and double check credentials of any possible music industry contact. Do not go to auditions or meetings alone and never allow yourself to be pressured into decisions. Any reputable contact will respect this and think more highly of you for doing things right!

The following information offers some general guidance and ideas for grabbing attention and creating opportunity on your path to success.

## *Gigging*

Gigging is a musician's term for getting out there in front of audiences and wowing them with your talent. A 'gig' can be anywhere from a local pub or theatre to a massive arena. Gigs are the perfect way for you to accrue valuable experience and, more importantly, build up a fan base. Those who think that a record company may spot them at a performance are sadly often misguided. Record company representatives (A&R) are extremely efficient at attending performances but will only do so if a 'buzz' is created about the artist. If a performance attracts huge audiences then you can rest assured that A&R people will know about it and attend. However, they will not drop into a small gig on the off-chance that they may find something.

Always try to generate lots of publicity for any performance. Try to generate local media interest. One of the best ways to increase your audience size is to sell (or even give away) CD's at each performance. Do not be tempted to try to make a huge profit on the sale of your initial CDs, as they are mainly a marketing tool. Hopefully more and more people will get to hear your work via the CDs and attend future performances. It would be fair to say that gigging is hard work and time consuming but, for performance experience alone, it is worth every moment to a serious performing artist.

## Management

If your budget allows, employing a manager or promoter is a great way to 'get yourself out there'. Make sure the person carrying out this work for you is experienced and has a keen interest in ensuring your success. Although friends and relatives may often offer to manage you, unless they are experienced in this field it would be wise to politely turn down these offers, as it may waste a lot of time and create disharmony between you. The best way to ensure a manager stays keen is to offer them a cut of your profit. This way they only get rich when you do. Please note that good managers are few and far between and will often be extremely expensive. This option is really only open to those who have a large initial budget.

## Social Networking Sites

There are many social networking websites available and many offer the opportunity to upload your own music to a profile page. Always ensure that only your very best work gets uploaded. These sites are regularly trawled by independent music reviewers and record company agents. Setting up your work on a social networking site is also a great way to introduce anyone you meet to your music – hopefully they will also direct others to it too.

## Creating a Demo

Every vocal performer will need to create recordings of their work for promotion. For this reason the chapter 'Recording A Demo' is solely dedicated to the creation of a demo and the process involved. When you are happy with your demo, get it to as many people as possible.

## Sending your work to record companies

This method of promotion has been the favourite method employed by new artists for years but it isn't always as successful as you may think - unless it is carried out in the right way. Record companies differ in the type of material that they deal with and a rock label, for example, will definitely not be interested in other types of work. It is essential that you do some research and find the record labels that are interested in the type of music that you perform. This can easily be achieved by internet searches and there are also many publications (make sure you get an up-to-date copy) that list record companies, producers and the genre they deal with.

Once you have found the right company to send your CD to, you then need to find the right people in the company. If you simply put your CD and covering letter in an envelope and send it as unsolicited mail it will probably just end up unheard and in the record company waste bin. Wherever possible, contact the record companies first (ideally by phone), and find out if they are willing to listen to your work. Get the right name and/or department to address the envelope to. This saves you time and money on CD production and postage and it also ensures your work has the best possible chance of being listened to. If possible, ask someone else to make the calls on your behalf. Not only does this make you sound like you have management, but it may also be far easier for someone else to sell you from an outsider's perspective.

## *Session Work*

Session work is when a singer/musician is employed to perform on a variety of material. This may include radio jingles, backing vocals and so on. Very seldom do you get a credit or great financial reward for this type of work but, you do get to meet producers and work in studios. Singers often regard this type of work as far from ideal. From personal experience, I can tell you that it is fun, challenging and a great way to meet a variety of industry professionals.

There are many more ways of creating opportunities and they change with time and technology. Be sure to research new ways of marketing yourself as an artist.

# Chapter completion checklist

Keep returning to the exercises in this chapter throughout your vocal development. You have successfully completed this chapter if you can agree with all of the statements below.

✓ I understand the need to be cautious when building music industry contacts

✓ I understand how 'Gigging' builds reputation and experience

✓ I understand that management can save time but is expensive

✓ I understand the need to get my material to as many people as possible using options including Social Networking websites

✓ I understand the 'best practice' for sending my work to others

✓ I am constantly researching new ways to promote myself

# YOUR NOTES

# YOUR NOTES

# YOUR NOTES

Chapter Twenty-One

# Recording A Demo

At some point in your career you will almost certainly be required to create a demo of your voice. This demonstration comprises a few PROFESSIONALLY recorded songs that show off your vocal ability. If a record company specifically asks for a demo, they will often give you guidance on what they require, however, if you are creating a demo for general promotion then it is best to follow the guidelines set out in this chapter.

A demo is not a full album of material and so would not be suitable to sell at gigs. In general, when creating a demo, you should not record any more than three or four songs. It is, after all, a demonstration of your ability and potential, not a finished album. You may already have many good recordings but do your best to whittle them down. A huge list of material will often put record companies off listening; they just want a taste of your best work. If there is interest in your work then you will be requested to send further material. Do not waste time and energy going for quantity, as it may be more of a disadvantage in your promotion efforts. As the old showbiz saying goes, "leave them wanting more!"

## What Should Be Included?

The material you include on your demo should give a good representation of your vocal ability. Ideally, it should demonstrate your vocal range, dynamic control and use of more than one resonating cavity (skills acquired in previous chapters). Carefully, choose songs that allow you to perform to your best ability whilst staying true to the identity of your performance (see 'The Fame Factor' chapter).

## Which Format?

Over the years there have been many fashionable types of media for creating demos including CD, Audio Tape, Mini-disc, DAT, MP3. It is always best to assume that the intended listener has the most basic equipment of the time and currently this would either be a CD player, or a computer to receive an email with MP3 attached. CD is the better option as it gives the listener something physical to receive and take notice of. CD players are also commonplace in vehicles, which may encourage a busy record company representative to test your sound during 'downtime' between meetings or on the way to the office. Ensure that your CD works in most CD players as some home CD-burners or brands of CD can be temperamental. If you choose the MP3 option, ensure that the MP3 settings allow for CD quality audio and minimum compression.

## *Where to Record*

Unless you have a wealth of recording and production experience, do not be tempted to 'do-it-yourself'. Use a professional studio setup and an experienced engineer. Good quality recording time can be relatively inexpensive when compared to several years ago. Small studios are cropping up everywhere as equipment becomes cheaper. When investigating studio options, ask to hear examples of previous work to ensure the quality is good. Ask the studios some questions about how they typically run a session and make sure there are no hidden costs (e.g. getting your work put onto CD or hiring microphones).

## *What to Expect During the Recording Session*

The following is a basic example of a typical studio recording process for voice and backing track only. This process may vary from studio to studio but the information set out here should assist 'first-timers' to be prepared and understand why each song takes a long time to record and mix.

* The engineer will load your backing track onto the recording system and check that it is playing correctly.

* You may be required to sing the song at this stage so that the engineer can determine what is required during the recording process.

* A good quality microphone will be selected to best suit your voice and the type of sound required for the genre of music. (Some studios use the same microphone for all recordings

and alter the sound afterwards).

✷ The engineer will test the level of your voice and the backing track. This usually involves singing the song with headphones on whilst settings are made on the recording equipment. You should ensure that you are able to clearly hear both your voice, and the music in your headphones. Headphones are used so that the backing music is not 'picked up' by the microphone. Other sound on the vocal track makes mixing the track more difficult. Singing with headphones can be a strange experience and you may wish to run through the song several times until you get used to how it sounds. You may be recorded in the same room as the engineer or be taken to another especially designed acoustic room or booth. Usually the engineer can communicate to you through the headphones in this situation.

✷ The recording can now begin. You can record the song in stages. This is useful if you need to re-record a section or line. You will not be expected to sing the song perfectly from beginning to end and many retakes are common (ensure you are well prepared so you can make the most of the studio time). Do not be afraid to tell the engineer if you go wrong or think you are not singing to the best of your ability. Go back and record sections as many times as required within the time constraints of the session.

✷ If required, the same process is repeated for backing vocals.

✷ Once the recording is complete, you will be able to listen to a rough mix of what you have recorded. This will not be a polished, finished product but it will allow you to hear if your performance is good. After this stage you may decide that some areas of the song need re-recording.

* The engineer will then work with the 'mix' of the song (some studios require the mix to happen at a later time as their ears may be less able to work optimally after listening hard in the recording process). This is where the levels of your vocal are set and any audio effects are added to enhance the sound.

* Once mixed, the track is prepared for burning onto CD. Ask if the recording data is saved at the studio in case you wish to make changes at a later date.

## Useful Technical Jargon

*Airy* – An instrument or voice that sounds like it is in a large sound reflective space

*Ambiance* – The audible sense of a room

*Attack* – The beginning of a note

*Automated Mixing* – A mixing desk that is programmed to adjust levels and effects automatically as the music is played

*Balance* –The relative volume levels of various tracks

*Bassy* – Having emphasised low frequency sound

*Bottom* – Low frequency sound

*Bounce Down* – To record several different tracks onto one track

*Boxy* – The sound quality is as if played inside a box

*Breathy* – Added airy sound to a voice or instrument

*Bright* – Emphasised high frequency

*Cans* – Headphones

**Channel** – A single path of audio e.g. one fader on a mixing desk for voice or guitar

**Chorus** – A sound effect that makes a single instrument or voice sound like it has multiplied

**Clean** – Free of effects or interference

**Compress** – A process to reduce the dynamic range

**Control Room** – Where the engineer works during a recording

**Cue Sheet** – A chronological list of mixer settings for a recording

**Dark** – Opposite of bright

**Decay** – The time it takes a note to end

**Decibel** – A unit of loudness

**De-esser** – A sound processor that removes or reduces sibilance

**Depth** – The audible sense of nearness

**Desk** – Mixing console/desk

**Distortion** – An intentional or unintentional change in audio quality leading to a degraded raspy quality

**Doubling** – To copy a recording and play both back (sometimes with a small delay on one) to give the effect of unison

**Drop in/out** – Sometimes called Punch In/Out - the process of recording over a section of previously recorded material by switching record on/off at designated times

**Dry** – No effects

**Dynamic Range** – The difference between loud and soft in a recording usually measured in decibels

**Echo** – A delayed repetition of sound

**Equalisation** – Adjustment of specific frequencies of sound

**Expander** – A process to increase the dynamic range of a recording

**Fade In** – To slowly and smoothly increase the volume

**Fade Out** – To slowly and smoothly decrease the volume

**Foldback** – A system to allow a previously recorded or live performance to be monitored through headphones

**Frequency** – The number of cycles per second of a sound wave measured in Hertz

**Gain** – Amplification - the difference in input signal to output signal

**Gate** – A device that shuts off the sound signal if the volume falls below a set volume

**Hard Disk Recording** – Recorded material is saved directly to a hard drive

**Hot** – Recording sound at high volume that causes mild distortion

**Input** – A connection going into a recording device

**Leakage** – Also known as 'Bleed' or 'Spill', the overlap of an instrument's sound into another instrument's microphone

**Level** – The degree of strength of a sound signal

**Limiter** – A device to stop sound from peaking and distorting

**Mask** – When one sound covers another

**Mixdown** – The process of playing all the separately recorded tracks together with the resultant sound sent to a stereo recorder

**Mixer** – Mixing desk/console

**Monitor** – Speakers used to monitor sound quality and balance

**Muddy** – Sound which lacks clarity

**Multitrack** – A device capable of recording more than two tracks

**Mute** – To silence a track

**Overdub** – To record over the top of other material

**Pan** – To control the level of sound coming from each speaker in a stereo

**Presence** – The sense of the sound being in the same room as the listener

**Reverb** – A common effect that gives the sound reflection as if in a specific room or hall - the reflections die out after the original sound has ended.

**Scratch Vocal** – A rough guide vocal in order to assist musicians or producers work with the track and is usually replaced

**Sibilance** – Excessive peaks in the frequency response in the 6-10kHz range due to an overemphasis of 's' and 'sh' sounds in a vocal recording

**Talkback** – The system used to allow the engineer to talk to the performer through headphones

***Take*** – A recorded performance - sometimes many takes are required to achieve the desired result

***Tracks*** – Separate locations for recordings usually containing a single channel of audio

# Chapter completion checklist

Keep returning to the exercises in this chapter throughout your vocal development. You have successfully completed this chapter if you can agree with all of the statements below.

✓  I understand the purpose of a demo

✓  I have carefully considered what should be included

✓  I have a good understanding of format options

✓  I understand the importance of a professional quality recording

✓  I know what to expect in a standard recording session

✓  I am familiar with a variety of studio jargon

# YOUR NOTES

Chapter Twenty-Two

# Preparing A Promotional Pack

A promotional pack is the ideal way to introduce yourself to record companies and agents. The pack will give a sample of your recorded work and also give a flavour of your overall identity as a performer. It is important that the pack looks professional and inspires the recipient to take notice. The following information gives guidance on the various elements you may wish to include. Not all elements are required. If you are not immensely proud of any one of the elements then do not include it.

## *Grab Attention!*

Before looking at some of the possible elements of your promo pack it is important to consider the importance of grabbing attention. How can you make your promo pack different and memorable? Record companies and agents receive literally thousands of promos every day and many will not get looked at. Try to find an unusual way of presenting your material to generate curiosity. Here are some examples of unusual presentation ideas for you to consider. These are just examples and you should try to be original in your approach:

1. Prepare your promotional material in something different to a standard envelope or package. I have seen promo material delivered in film reel cans and many other types of novelty cases. This grabs attention and everyone in the record company office will be intrigued as to what it is.

2. Include useful items in your promo pack. This can range from personalised pens to chocolate and will ensure someone looks at the pack. Everyone likes a free gift!

3. If you are creative, try to think of new ways of presenting your information. This might be anything from an interesting folder design to a unique computer presentation.

ENSURE YOUR UNIQUE IDEAS ARE PRACTICAL AND ACCES-SIBLE – i.e. a gramophone record would be a unique way of presenting your work but very few people could play it.

## *Recorded Material*

Your recording will probably be delivered in CD format. Remember that recordable media is available in a variety of shapes and sizes and an unusual design will grab more attention. Ensure that the songs included on the CD are of a high standard and check your CD on various players to ensure it plays properly. If your budget allows, get your CD professionally printed. There are also many cheaper 'DIY' solutions for labelling your CD. Ensure that the CD label includes your contact information in case the disc gets separated from the rest of the pack. It is also a good idea to put the track details on the disc for the same reason. As mentioned in the 'Recording a Demo' chapter, it is best not to put too many tracks on the CD. Make sure your CD is in some sort of case and not loose in the pack as it may get scratched and damaged. The CD case does not have to be printed, but if you decide to create a CD booklet, remember that text is often not noticed, as a large percentage of people do not read all the text on CD cases.

## *Cover Letters*

Cover letters are important to establish a reason for the promotional pack. Keep all covering letters brief but include the following information:

Recipient Name (if known)

Your contact details

Reason for sending e.g. it has been requested or you are currently looking for management

Next step e.g. you would love the opportunity to meet with the company/agent

Thank you – always remember to thank the recipient for their time

# CV

A traditional CV is rarely required for a promo pack but the typical information that a CV would hold should be presented in an exciting way. This information should include interests/hobbies and performance experience/ music training. Remember a vocal performer is an all-round entertainer and must have personality in order to become a 'product' that a record company can promote and sell. Life experience information is an important part of your complete package and should always be included. Keep the information brief, interesting, unusual and well presented. In-depth information can be given if further details are requested as a result of sending the promo package.

## Photos

Do not send your holiday snaps! Photographs are vital and must be of a professional standard. Before rushing to book your photo session, remember to think about your performance identity and ensure the photos reflect this. You will need copyright free pictures if you want to use them digitally or make your own copies. Discuss this with your photographer. Most photographers are happy to discuss your needs and may be able to offer you suggestions for poses. Explain what style of photo you are aiming for. Remember, this is not a school portrait. Ensure photos are unique enough to sell you!

## Video

There are typically two types of promo video for new artists. The first is a live performance video. A live performance video is recorded with a live audience in order to make clear that the performance is real. After several performances (or gigs) you will be able to gauge which songs an audience react well to. This will enhance your status as a performer. Be sure to use the best possible camera that your budget will allow. Audio is usually recorded separately and then edited in-sync with the visual later. If possible, hire a professional to record your performance.The second type of video is a fully-produced music video. This is more complex and will be a longer, more expensive process. Audio from a recording session is used and the video footage is overlaid, usually with some lip-sync.

For both types of video, ensure that your identity as a performer is obvious. There are many ways of presenting a video piece including DVD and various computer formats. Speak to your videographer to discuss the current options.

## Performance Invites

If you are actively performing on a regular basis, it is a good idea to include your performance dates along with an invitation to attend. Ensure that any performances that you are extending invitations to are high profile and/or well attended, as audience reaction will play a large role in an agent's opinion of your future potential.

# Chapter completion checklist

Keep returning to the exercises in this chapter throughout your vocal development. You have successfully completed this chapter if you can agree with all of the statements below.

✓ I understand the purpose of a promotional pack

✓ I am aware of possible techniques to ensure my promo pack is unique and interesting

✓ I understand how to prepare and label my recorded material

✓ I understand the importance of integrating my performance image into the package via written and visual means

✓ I will not include any material that I am not proud of

# YOUR NOTES

# Chapter Twenty-Three

# FAQ

This chapter aims to answer frequently asked questions. Most questions can be addressed by reviewing the specific information given in each chapter. Below are genuine questions asked by singing students:

Q: What is the most important element when learning to sing?

A: If you ask several teachers (or singers) you will receive many different answers. The truth is that everyone is different. The important elements at different points of your personal development will vary. Although breathing is generally considered to be the main element to master (as it provides the raw ingredient for sound), some people will have good air control and so another element will be more important to them. Working through this book in chapter order will help you build upon all the elements successfully.

Q: How do I know if I'm using the correct resonating cavity?

A: Experience will allow you to instinctively know which is best. When you practise use of the resonating cavities, ensure they are so well mastered that they no longer feel strange. If you are experienced enough with the cavities, you will naturally place the sound without too much thought. Initially, you may have to try all the resonances and gauge which is the best fit for the performance. A Dictaphone or other basic recording device is very useful for this.

Q: How long should I spend practising each chapter?

A: Ideally, you should practise each day and not move on until you are comfortable that you have mastered every detail of the chapter. Most chapters will require at least one week of daily practice (rushing through chapters will result in little or no physical development).

Q: I have a cold which is affecting my sound but I still want to practise...is that ok?

A: Whilst I congratulate you on your commitment to practise, I would strongly advise that you recover from illness before continuation of practice. Putting additional stress on the body could result in vocal damage, bad practice, disheartenment and prolonged duration of the illness.

Q: Why do I get a dry throat when I practise?

A: This is a common problem and usually caused by 'over-blowing' on notes. If your breathing is incorrect and too-much air is used, the throat can quickly dry out. Check to see if there is any audible hiss (air escaping noise) when holding notes and generally throughout your singing. Review the information on breathing or try allowing a little air out before singing each phrase. Constant over-blowing can cause discomfort and in some cases long-term damage to the voice. Until this is rectified, ensure your practice is carried out in short blocks rather than over a long uninterrupted period.

Q: Does stress affect singing?

A: YES! Stress can affect your state of mind, confidence, posture, vocal muscle control and breathing! Ensure that when you practise you are as relaxed as possible. Singing should be enjoyable, even when you get things wrong! If you are stressed in any way, make every effort to rectify this before practice. Some students find that professional massage or osteopath visits help their overall sound and practice.

Q: What equipment should I purchase to aid my learning?

A: You can successfully complete this book without any additional purchases. It may, however, be of use to have a good quality sound system to play any backing tracks or original songs. The playing of songs through small speakers (i.e. a laptop computer) is not recommended as there tends to be inadequate low frequency sound in which to get a good sense of the vocal balance within the music. If you use a laptop, it would be useful to purchase some good quality additional speakers. A Dictaphone or other recording device (i.e. mobile phone voice recorder) is also useful to monitor your practice. It is good to keep initial recordings so that you can keep track of your improvement. A Dictaphone helps us to hear what the audience hears. Often what we consider to be a strange sound to make will be a good sound to hear and this can be missed without recorded proof.

Q: Where can I obtain backing tracks?

A: By far the most cost effective way of obtaining backing tracks is to search online music download providers. Most of the major music sites have a selection of karaoke tracks available to purchase individually in mp3 format. Karaoke CDs can also be purchased from most high street music shops. Shops may need to order your required song/karaoke abum.

Q: What's the best way to prepare for an audition?

A: Audition requirements vary greatly depending on the type of audition. Ensure you have all the information possible to be fully prepared. If an audition requires a small section of a song to be sung, learn the whole thing anyway. Stick to just the required section in the audition but ensure you are prepared to do more if asked. Have a few other songs in various styles practised in case the audition panel ask for more. Even if other songs are not stated as being required in the pre-audition info, it can happen, so be prepared. Ensure you carefully plan your route to any audition and aim to be there a little early so there is no risk of ruining your chances by arriving late. Always be friendly and polite to both staff and other people taking the audition. Often you are judged on your social skills and ability to beworked with, as well as your talent.

Q: I have been practising everyday for a long period, but don't seem to be improving – why is this?

A: First, check your understanding of what is to be practised. It is important that you do not just practise technique that you can easily do. Many people do not notice their own improvement as it can be a gradual change. Ensure you keep recordings of your voice throughout your development, so that you can be surprised by just how much you have really achieved!

Q: I have improved and feel I have a good understanding of the techniques, where can I learn more?

A: Everywhere! Watch performers and work out what they are doing. Research all available techniques with an open mind. There are many other books and courses available covering a wide variety of views. Not all material you find will be good, but even the bad can help you reach important decisions about what is really of value. Check the internet regularly for singing information. The only voice teachers to be cautious of are those who suggest that their approach is the ONLY approach.

# GLOSSARY

**A & R**
Artist and Repertoire. A division of a record label that takes responsibility for scouting new talent and developing artists.

**Acoustic**
a. The science of sound.
b. An instrument that does not produce or affect sound electronically.

**Ad-lib**
Ad libitum. An indication to improvise.

**Booth**
A sound-proofed area designed to keep internal sound in and external sound out.

**Bridge**
a. A musical interlude that connects two parts of a song.
b. The transition area between two resonating cavities of the voice. Also called passagio or break.

**Cavity**
A space in which sound can resonate.

**Compression**
An electronic process to reduce the dynamic range of sound.

**Compression** (on MP3 and other audio)
Reduction in the file size of audio.

**Diaphragm**
The muscle that separates the chest cavity from the abdomen. The diaphragm is the main muscle of respiration.

**Genre**
A type or style of music (e.g. Pop, Rock, Classical).

**High Frequency**
A high pitched sound.

**Input Signal**
A signal going into an electronic system (e.g. a microphone signal into an amplifier).

**Larynx (Voice box)**
Part of the respiratory tract. It contains the vocal cords.

**Legato**
In a smooth even style.

**Low Frequency**
A low pitched sound.

**Melody**
A succession of notes that create a musical phrase.

**Musicality**
Musical sensitivity or talent.

**Output Signal**
A signal going out of an electronic system (e.g. the signal from an amplifier to the speakers).

**Peaking**
When an audio signal becomes too loud. This may cause distorted sound.

**Pharynx**
The hollow space that extends from the mouth and nose to the larynx.

**Pick up**
A device that converts sound into an electronic signal.

**Pitch**
The measure of how high or low a note is.

**Reflection**
The repetition of sound resulting from sound waves bouncing from surfaces (i.e. echo or reverb).

**Resonance**
The intensification and prolongation of sound due to vibrations created within the body of an object (e.g. acoustic guitar body or human chest cavity). A ringing quality.

**Rhythm**
The pattern of musical movement (beat).

**Sibilance**
A hiss. Usually produced on 's' or 'sh' sounds.

**Staccato**
Short detached parts or sounds.

**Technique**
The method or manner of performance.

**Timbre**
The qualities of a sound that distinguish it from other sounds.

**Tone**
The quality of vocal or musical sound.

**Tune**
a. A melody.
b. To properly adjust pitch.

**Vibrato**
A tremulous or pulsating vocal effect.

**Vocal Cords**
Two small bands of muscle within the larynx. These muscles vibrate to produce the voice.